The District

Growing Up in Little Italy

a memoir by Rose Grieco

Library and Archives of Canada Cataloguing in Publication

Grieco, Rose

      The District: Growing Up in Little Italy

ISBN 978-0-9948813-0-4

Editor: Larry Hicock

Editorial consulting and proofreading: Pat Zanatta, Victoria Zielinski, and Christina Grieco

Cover and book design: Sparketers, Toronto

Back cover photo: Marilyn Ariosa

Printed in the United States of America

Published in Canada by The Gypsy Press

First edition 2015

The Gypsy Press
Toronto Ontario Canada

Acknowledgements

I'd like first and foremost to acknowledge all the love and support I received from my late husband Vic while I was writing this book. I could not have done it without his encouragement.

A special thanks to my children Patricia Zanatta, Victoria and Chris Zielinski (son-in-law) and my grandchildren Christina Grieco and Jordan Zanatta (website design) for all their work in helping me share my story with all of you. Thanks to all my grandchildren for listening to my stories over and over again and never growing tired of hearing them.

A special wish of gratitude to my editor and book designer, Larry Hicock and his partner Irene at Sparketers, for all their support, knowledge and hard work. They gave me the courage and guidance I needed to get my story published.

I am grateful to the many, many friends and family who encouraged me along the way and helped me in many different ways, including Joe Vertolli, Mary Ciampini, Mary Ann Rowlands, Marcus Lepkowski, Jack Kirchhoff (retired former deputy book editor, The Globe and Mail), Peter Collini, Agata Bochenek, Mary Asbil and Michelle Breslin. And many thanks to everyone who shared their photos with me, including Heather Duncan, Paula Greco, Eddie Jackson, Mike Grimaldi, Carlo Bigelli, Leonard and Grace Lombardi, and the late Willie Antonacci.

We have made every effort to be as accurate as possible regarding names, dates and events. I accept full responsibility for any errors or omissions.

A tribute to all the characters...

This book is dedicated to the lovable characters I grew up with – the wheelers and dealers, the kibitzers, the shit disturbers – and most of all to our immigrant parents, who had the strength and survival instinct to make it work in this new and strange country. Their hard discipline and tough love instilled in us the importance of family and responsibility. Together they all helped to create the ambience and camaraderie of our great neighbourhood. You are gone but never forgotten. You all live on in our memories.

For my family

The District

Growing Up in Little Italy

When I first thought about writing a book, my intention was to write about the magic of cooking, in frugal times, with whatever we had. I learned how to cook at a very young age. Being the second oldest girl in a family of ten children, I certainly had to do my share. But thinking back on my life – growing up in Little Italy, the struggles of our immigrant parents, what they had to endure during those lean years and surviving them with dignity – I decided I should write about our neighbourhood. I believe there will never be a neighbourhood like ours was, back in those early days.

The camaraderie that existed was unlike anything you will ever see anywhere. I really believe that our children and our grandchildren deserve a taste of that way of life. Had I known at an early age that I would be writing a book, I would have kept a diary, but now in my declining years, I have to rely on memories.

* * *

I was born and raised in Toronto. My parents came from Italy. My father came from a little town way up in the Gran Sasso mountainous region of Abruzzo called Campotosto, in the province of L'Aquila. My mother was born in Vita, in the province of Trapani in Sicily.

Riccardo Vertolli came to Canada in June of 1913 on the ship, Re D'Italia. He boarded in a house on Treford Place in Toronto. His brothers, who came to Canada before him, helped him settle in. My mother, Josephine Antonia Giorlando, came over with her parents, Antonia and Luciano, and her brother Mario in February of 1920, on the S.S. Belvedere.

What would possess them to leave their place of birth, their country and their roots? How bad could the situation have been for thousands of immigrants to leave their homeland and come to a strange new country half way across the world, not knowing what the future would hold? Suffice it to say, unemployment, low wages and disease. In other words, as you hear so often from immigrants, "la miseria."

In the case of my maternal grandparents, their troubles began with the dreaded phylloxera disease, which wiped out the vineyards in Vita. Many of the village people, including my grandfather, took their families to Tunisia to work the vineyards there. My mother used to tell us stories about living in Tunisia. She remembered, as young as she was, playing with the little black children, which she'd never seen before, and pinching them to see if it hurt them like it hurt her. My grandfather used to tell us of the eels that the townspeople would hang up. When the maggots began to form on them, they were ready to eat. As young children we would cringe at the thought of it, and he would laugh at our reactions. I sometimes wonder if he was telling the truth or just telling stories.

Eventually, the phylloxera disease spread to Tunisia and wiped out the vineyards there. Now back in Vita, my grandparents had to make some big decisions. Finally they decided to go the way of the many thousands who had emigrated before them. They made their way to the

United States and then to Canada, probably with the help of a network of labour agents or *padroni*, who found a place for them to stay when they arrived. Perhaps some of their townspeople who were already here helped set them up in a boarding house. Living in a boarding house was a way of life back then for the immigrants, although for some of them it didn't take long to branch out on their own. They were resourceful and they were hard workers. When they were able to buy a house of their own, they rented part of it to help pay the mortgage. To own a home was their dream.

* * *

The first major influx of Italian immigrants that came over at the turn of the century had settled in the "Ward" – the College-Queen-Yonge-University area, which in the late 1800s was called St. John's Ward. They helped build the downtown core, from the roads and sewers to the streetcar tracks and hospitals. They came to this country and into a society that didn't really accept them. They lived in crowded rooming houses and worked under terrible conditions. They did not have the safe working standards that are compulsory today. Being in a strange country, you certainly would not complain to the foreman for fear of losing your job. They were being discriminated against and were perceived as uneducated, ignorant people with low IQs but strong backs.

Did they think all Italians were ignorant? Had they forgotten the great explorers, like Christopher Columbus, Giovanni Caboto or Amerigo Vespucci? The inventors, like Marconi and Leonardo Da Vinci? The artists, like Michelangelo, Botticelli and Donatello? The scientists, like Galileo, Volta or Torricelli? The singers, like Enrico Caruso or Beniamino Gigli?

According to John E. Zucchi's book, "Italians in Toronto", Italians started immigrating to Toronto as early as the 1800s. One of the first settlers was Philip DeGrassi, a Roman-born British Imperial officer. James Forneri, a Piedmontese, was the University of Toronto's professor of modern languages; he arrived in 1853. Francesco Rossi was the first ice cream and confection maker; in the 1830s he catered to the King and Bay area. Angelo Belfonti opened the first Italian restaurant, Angelo's, on Elm Street near Bay Street, in 1922. I believe this area was probably the first "Little Italy", and Angelo's was one of the first of many Italian restaurants that followed.

Many of the Italian immigrants might not have had an education but they had dignity and fierce pride. All they wanted to do was earn a living and save a few bucks. If these same people who discriminated against them were to listen in on their conversations at the end of their hard day's work — to hear of their dreams, waiting for the day when they could send for their families—then maybe, just maybe, they would think differently. (And besides, who *are* the true Canadians? Anybody who sailed across the ocean to get to America was an immigrant, be it on the Mayflower or the S.S. Belvedere or the Re D'Italia.) Actually, had it not been for the immigrants of various nationalities who helped build this great city, I daresay we might still be using outhouses!

When the Great Depression hit and there were no jobs to be had, they did what they had to do to survive. Some of them bootlegged to stay off of the relief system, and in doing so they were later able to send their children to university. Some of the children grew up to become doctors, lawyers, politicians and fine upstanding citizens... and some became mobsters. Some immigrants, their spirit broken by constant illness and unemployment, returned to their homeland. Others moved out of the Ward and settled around Dundas and Grace Street, where St. Agnes Roman Catholic Church was situated. Already there had been an influx of Italians who'd settled here, and this is the area that would later become what we know today as Little Italy.

* * *

Little Italy was a town within a city. It spanned from just south of Dundas Street to just north of College Street, and from the east at Euclid Avenue west to Montrose Avenue. The College Street area has become very trendy, especially around Clinton and College, where the

Mastrangelo family opened the Bar Diplomatico almost 50 years ago; it continues to be a favourite place to meet. Another favourite is Sicilian Ice Cream, which was opened at College and Montrose in 1959 by the Galipo Brothers. With their outside tables and chairs, they introduced the "café" ambience along College Street.

Other venues soon followed, such as Il Gatto Nero and the Standard Pizza and Pasta Bar at College and Beatrice, formerly the Standard Club; this was a popular spot to meet your friends and raise a glass of suds and sing along to war songs and the songs of that era. They had a projector with a pull-down screen showing all of the words to the songs and everybody would join in. A few guys would get together in the back to play a card game like *Briscola*, and everybody always seemed to be having a great time.

When I was a teenager in the 40s, these were our stomping grounds. We walked around without fear, we slept on our verandas on hot summer nights, and we never locked our doors. I once read in a magazine, the name of which I have long since forgotten, that College Street was chosen as one of the top five unique areas in all of North America. As I walk along College today and see all of the changes that have been made over the years, I can't help but think about how it was way back then, when I was young. I get a warm and comforting feeling, because even though times were tough, there was always this sense of belonging. In my neighbourhood, you knew everybody.

* * *

It didn't take long for my parents to meet, as they lived on the same street, but my maternal grandparents would not allow my father to see my mother. You see, on the ship coming over from Italy, a young man of means who was on his way to New York had wanted to marry my mother, but she wasn't having any of it. My mother was a very strong-willed person and did not give in to her parents' wishes to marry the man from the ship, who'd continued to pursue her.

My parents decided that they were going to get married no matter what. My Uncle Ernest, the eldest of my father's brothers, went to my grandparents' house to tell them that my parents planned to marry and that they wanted their blessing and wanted them to attend the wedding. My grandfather replied, "I will attend the wedding and bring my shotgun," to which my uncle replied, "And I will be waiting with my gun!" Of course, these were only words, and nothing ever came of it.

On October 11th, 1920, my parents eloped. It must have taken a lot of guts to do this, coming from a strict Sicilian family, but I guess love conquers all. It was a good thing that she was strong-willed, because her life to follow was to be anything but easy.

Mamma moved into Pa's rented room on Treford Place. And so began a long history of many moves and many children. In 1921, they rented their first home at 18 Clinton Street, where their first child, Louie, was born. In 1923 they moved to 9 Treford Place, where Louie managed to crawl out of the second floor window and fall to the ground below. Fortunately he did not suffer any permanent damage. Their second son, Luciano, was born here. Just a year later, in 1924, they moved to 268 Claremont Street where their first daughter, Pat, was born. In 1926, after five years of renting and moving from house to house, they were able to buy their first home, at 502 Manning Avenue. It was here that my brother Ernie, myself, and my sister Eleanor were each born.

* * *

I was born in 1928. I was the fifth child and the second girl. As young as I was, I remember the happy times in that house — my father slicing the homemade salami and prosciutto, because it always seemed that we had company, my uncles or our *paesans* – and mostly I remember sitting on my grandmother's knee.

I also remember some of the songs of that era. We owned a Victrola, and along with all of our Italian records, my parents listened to these English songs, like "When You and I Were Young, Maggie", "Oh Where, Oh Where, Has My Little Dog Gone?", "Where Have You Been Billy Boy, Billy Boy?" and "The Last Rose of Summer". And then there was this laughing record they played – that's all it was, people laughing constantly throughout the whole record – and pretty soon everybody in the room would be laughing hysterically. I think it would be a good idea for this record to be played in seniors' homes. I find that very strange now thinking about it – my parents being so Italian and listening to all of those English records. I remember my father singing "Roamin' in the Gloamin'" in his broken English ("Roamin' ina da Gloamin'"). And also "Hallelujah, I'm a Bum", and "K-K-K-Katy". I guess he picked them up from his co-workers in construction.

* * *

But things changed. With the Great Depression and the "Dirty Thirties", there were no jobs to be had. So when any of the Italian immigrants lost their homes, you can imagine the heartbreak and frustration that they experienced, having to go back to square one. But they were survivors.

My father went to Kirkland Lake, where two of his brothers lived, and he was able to find work in the mines. In the meantime, my mother tried hard to survive here. In 1931, the year my sister Eleanor was born, things got even worse and, in 1932, we lost our home. I was very young at that time, but I remember Mamma talking to the man who held her mortgage, asking him to give her more time to pay him (my father was arranging to send money home to her), but he refused. His face is etched into my memory, and every time I see a movie villain with dark hair and moustache, it brings me back to that day.

So, we had to move again. I remember my mother packing small items in the baby carriage with me holding onto the side. We walked several times back and forth, moving our things to 272 Claremont Street, where my brother Joe was born. That same year, we moved to 288 Manning Avenue, and then in 1935 to 22 Treford Place.

It was here that I started school, at the age of six. (There was no kindergarten then.) It was here, too, that I made my First Holy Communion. I remember this well because I was the centre of attention, and being singled out and fussed over in a large family didn't happen very often, except if you were a baby. Babies were always the centre of attention. Another happy memory was when my brother Ernie and I were told that we had to have our tonsils removed. We were so happy because we knew we would be eating ice cream all week. In those days it was required that you eat ice cream after a tonsillectomy, and the neighbours would bring bricks of ice cream for us. When my father took us on the streetcar to St. Joseph's Hospital for our operation, you would think that we were going on a vacation. How different things are today. In those days, if you had a bad cold you stayed in bed with a mustard plaster on your chest and back, and a neighbour would come and visit, and maybe bring you some soup or fruit. Visiting sick neighbours was like a social event. Today you take an Aspirin or Tylenol and get on with it.

In thinking about Treford Place, I remember all of the fun we had, although it didn't take much to make us happy. There was this man called "Mauromil", who lived with the Cappuccitti family on the corner of Treford and Claremont (which is now California Sandwiches). He was a one-man band; he played the mouth organ and had musical instruments attached to his knees, and all the kids on the street danced around him. He had stubble on his face and wore a tattered hat. Today that might be considered quite stylish.

The young boys in the neighbourhood formed a band and called themselves the Columbus Club Boys Band. They paraded up and down the streets playing their makeshift instruments, and us kids would all run out to the street and watch them walk by and then we would follow them.

And how excited we were when the Jewish High Holidays came. A Jewish family, the Miskins, lived on the corner of Treford and Bellwoods and they would pay Salvina Roberto and me a penny to light the gas stove or to turn on a light for them. One penny bought us a grab bag, and what a thrill it was anticipating the contents. And then there were the Saturday matinees at the Duchess Theatre on Dundas Street. For five cents we saw a double feature, news of the week, cartoons, and a serial. When they raised admission to six cents we couldn't go, but that only lasted a few weeks. I guess my mother decided it was worth the extra penny to get us out of her hair for a few hours.

I remember one Christmas week when I was six or seven years old and my uncles came down from Kirkland Lake to visit. They were bachelors and they wore spats and looked very dapper indeed. They were always treated like royalty. One night they gave my brother Ernie and me a nickel each. That night felt extremely joyous, with the smell of anisette biscotti that my mother baked every Christmas, and the happy atmosphere in the house. I went outside and the sky was midnight blue and loaded with stars, and the snow was crisp and shone like diamonds. It was almost magical. Christmas was in the air and I had a nickel in my pocket. Life was beautiful.

We loved when my uncles came to visit. It didn't matter that we had to give up our beds and sleep on the floor on blankets. It was fun and we always knew they were good for a couple of pennies or a chocolate bar. Usually when my uncles were visiting, all of the *paesans* would get together and go to my Uncle Henry's garage, which was just across the lane from our back yard. Uncle Henry played his homemade bagpipes (*zampogna*) and they would all drink homemade wine and sing. My mother didn't mind them having a good time, but she hated when my father came home 'feeling good'.

One day she went to Uncle Henry's house and asked him not to give my father any wine. Well, that was a real no-no for a wife to do, especially a Campotostaro's wife. It sure did not sit too well with my father – something to do with his "macho manhood" – but my mother didn't care. She spoke her mind. One day, when my father had his brothers and a few *paesans* over for a game of *Briscola*, he said to my mother, "Uaglio, prenda mi 'na birra, e se no," which loosely translated means, "Bring me a beer, or else," in a manner that suggested an immediate response. Well, my mother, who was cooking nearby, just happened to have a knife in her hand and went right up to my father and said, "Or else, what?!" Another no-no. Well, my father made light of it and started to laugh because my uncles told him off. They had a lot of respect for my mother. As a matter of fact, in Campotosto, where my father was born, whenever any of the townspeople who'd immigrated to Canada passed away here, they would ring the church bells, so that all of the people in the village would soon know. When my mother passed in 1986, my first cousin Livio (who first met my mother when they visited us in 1980) rang the bells for her, even though she was not from Campotosto.

We had our share of sad memories. In 1935, my mother gave birth to a baby girl.

Our Baby was born in '35

She lived one day and then she died

Her life on earth was not to be

For reasons only known to He.

She was a beautiful baby. I can still picture her in a white dress and bonnet with white ribbons, lying in a little white coffin on a velvet couch at Moffatt's Funeral Parlour on College Street.

Another terrible memory was when my brother Ernie and my cousin George were trying to make a slingshot with a wire hanger and a tire band. Unfortunately, something went terribly wrong and George lost an eye. He had to have a glass eye, earning him the name "Hawkeye", which stayed with him for the rest of his life.

The Depression and its effects lasted a long time; economically speaking, times were still not good. In 1936 my sister Joanie was born. Eventually we had to go on relief, now known as welfare. I recall my mother taking some of us kids to Trinity Bellwoods Park. We would all pick dandelions and sit there and clean them and we would each take a bag to carry home. Some of these she would preserve for the winter. My grandfather used to go and pick mushrooms with a big sack on his back. He would take a streetcar somewhere, probably no further than Eglinton Avenue, as there was a lot of open space up there in those years. My mother would spend hours cleaning the mushrooms and she would preserve some for the winter, too. When she cooked the mushrooms she would put a quarter in the pan and if it turned black, that meant that the mushrooms were poisonous, but it never did turn black.

I will never forget one incident, when the relief inspector came to our house. He looked in every room and when he went down to the cellar, he saw that my mother had some preserves on the shelf. He said to my parents, "Oh, you people have food here, I am cutting you off of relief." My mother just stared at him and didn't say a word. The look on her face said it all. My father literally picked him up and shoved him out the door saying, "You *somanabitch* you, don't ever come back to this house again!"

I mean, people didn't come to Canada to bilk the relief system. These were hard working people. They wanted to work. They would work at anything and they *did* work at anything. They did all the rotten jobs that the people here wouldn't do, and for them to be on relief was beneath their dignity. Don't get me wrong; they appreciated all of the help that was given to them. That inspector never did come back and the one who took his place was a lot nicer. Oh I know you might wonder, why did they keep on having children if times were so bad? For one thing, they were Catholics, and besides, there was no birth control pill in those days. And even if there was, would she have taken it? I do not know. And heaven forbid an Italian man wear a condom – fuggedaboutit!

Most of us kids on Treford Place did not have the opportunity to go to college or university. One exception was Joseph Chiappetta; he had the luxury of going to university and became a very fine lawyer.

Some of us couldn't even go to high school, but we managed to make a very good living – for example, in the food and beverage business.

Louis Jannetta, who lived next door to me, had to leave school after grade eight to go to work. He started as a busboy and worked his way up to being the maître d' at the very popular Imperial Room in the Royal York Hotel. He worked there for 35 years. He later wrote a book entitled *"King of the Maitre D's: My Life Among the Stars"*. Ralph Trauzzi got a job at the King Edward Hotel and worked his way up to being the manager of room service. Corry (his last name I've never known) became head chef at the infamous Town Tavern, where Max Bluestein was brutally beaten by friends of a mob boss, John Papalia, from Hamilton. Freddie Maddalena also had to leave school and go to work. He started as a busboy at the King Edward Hotel, and later at the Club One Two, where he then became the maître 'd'. When the club closed its doors, he went to work at the Barclay Hotel. Eventually he moved to California and operated fine restaurants and is now retired.

I also worked in the restaurant industry, at the Club One Two, the La Scala dining room, and the Blue Orchid supper club (now Lee's Palace). I later opened my own restaurant called Mama Rosa's, which I operated for 17 years.

* * *

Thinking of Treford Place in those years of our lives, I recall mostly happy memories. After all, surviving the Depression was a way of life, and it was my parents' problem, not ours. We children didn't know we were poor — it was just the way things were.

In 1937, we moved to Montrose Avenue and I remember that it was there that my Aunt Rose Orlando, my mother's first cousin, gave us our first radio. Boy, what a thrill it was to have a radio. We surrounded it like it was some kind of god. My sister Pat really loved it. Just entering her teens, she liked singers like Russ Columbo, and then Bing Crosby, and she would be absolutely glued to it. She started high school at that time and sometimes she would play hooky because she was ashamed of some of her clothes. Especially the brown felt dress with the big orange balls, which was later handed down to me. I wasn't as brave as Pat. As much as I tried to get out of wearing that awful-looking dress, I was made to wear it; everybody called it a pogey dress.

My Aunt Rose had two daughters, Nina and Anna, and sometimes she would give us some of their clothes, which were really nice. She owned a grocery store on Yonge Street called Orlando's. (When Pat and I were a little older we went to work at the store on Saturdays. We really enjoyed working there, especially at lunchtime. We had a choice of cold cuts for our sandwiches. Aunt Rose was very kind. On Saturday night when we finished work, she always gave us some fruit and vegetables to bring home. At that time, the war was on. Nina's husband Gord was in the service and was called for active duty. The night he left was a Saturday, and we all came over to say our goodbyes. Nina used to write him every day. She would send him all kinds of goodies. Then the terrible news came: Gord had been killed in action.)

1937 was also the year C.B.C. Radio introduced the "Happy Gang". It was one of C.B.C.'s first popular programs. It featured variety programming and comedy, and it aired from 1:00 p.m. to 1:30 p.m., Monday to Friday. Approximately two million people tuned in. They started their program, led by Bert Pearl, Bob Farnon, Kay Stokes and Blain Mathe, with their signature introduction, "Knock Knock. Who's there? It's the Happy Gang. Well, come on in." Most of the students in our school lived close by and went home for lunch. Some of them got hooked on the Happy Gang and were late getting back to school. Needless to say, they were reprimanded and/or strapped.

In 1938 we moved to 221 Bellwoods. This was by far the worst scenario. It was a small wartime-type bungalow, with three little bedrooms and one very small room that served as our living room/ dining room/kitchen. A small back shed, the size of a closet, housed a toilet. There were no bathtubs. We took our baths in a galvanized tub once a week. I also remember my mother doing a lot of cooking in the back yard.

By this time there were eight of us children. The three older boys, Lou, Slim and Ernie, slept in one room on a double bed. My sisters Pat, Eleanor and I, along with my brother Joe, slept in the other room, also on a double bed. There were no queen- or king-sized beds then. We really felt like sardines in a can. My sister Joanie was lucky. She had a crib all to herself. I remember the bickering we did when we went to bed, such as, "Stop hogging all the blankets!" or "Move over, I'm falling off the bed!" or some other such nonsense, until my father would come into the room and warn us to be quiet and go to sleep. Of course we didn't and we would keep it up. Finally my father would come into our room and whack us with the strap. It didn't matter who did the bickering, we all got whacked, and we would cover ourselves with a blanket and pretend he was hurting us. When he left the room we would all start laughing. At this time, as if things were not crowded enough, my sister Gloria was born. She inherited the crib and Joanie slept with my parents.

I was ten years old then and I remember thinking, "Is this what life is all about, my mother being pregnant and having babies?" But all in all, us kids had lots of fun. There were always enough kids outside to play with. One of my friends always managed to have a little money on her, which was unusual in those days. Her mother did a little bootlegging on the side to help during tough times, and hid the money in the grandfather clock. My friend knew this and "borrowed" some of the money. We used to go to Jack's Cigar Store on Dundas and Euclid and she would buy candy and gum and share them with me. It was always exciting: when you bought one stick of gum and unwrapped it, if the gum was black, you would win a whole package of Wrigley's.

There were also sad days. One day my friend Salvina's mother was going to the hospital to have her appendix out. What was supposed to be a simple appendectomy turned tragic and she died. Her death sent shockwaves through the neighbourhood and especially through her family, leaving her husband and eight children without a wife and mother. The youngest child was just fifteen months old. Marianna, the eldest, who was deaf, nevertheless took over raising her siblings, three of which were partially blind. Aside from all her responsibilities, Marianna found a diversion. She would disappear for an hour or so and her father would be looking for her, wondering where she was. She would be up the lane near DiLeo's lumberyard shooting craps with the best of them. This bunch included, "Beaky" Pesce, John "Dusty" DiLeo, Peter Zambri and Bertie Mignacco. God love her, Marianna was a real trooper.

In 1939 we moved to 260 Claremont Street, a three-story, eight-room house. It was like moving into a palace, and it was a good thing we moved into this big house because in 1940 my sister Mary was born. I thought, "Oh no, not another baby to watch!"

I will never forget that day. It was early morning and my mother was going through terrible labour pains. The doctor, Isabella Wood, hadn't arrived yet. My grandmother ("Nonna") was at her side and through my mother's guidance, she delivered the baby. My father was crying to see my mother suffer so. My Uncle Ernest, who was visiting at the time, was giving my father hell, saying, "Basta, she's had enough!"

I couldn't take it. I ran out of the house and ran to my girlfriend Frances Crimo's house on Henderson Avenue. I told Mrs. Crimo what was happening at home. She was my mother's *paesan* from Sicily. After a while I went back home. My sister Pat was keeping the small children away from the bedroom, assuring them that Mamma was going to be all right. Well after all that, we stood around the crib looking at our new baby sister, each one of us commenting on who she looked like. We were counting her fingers and toes, while Pat and my mother were deciding on a name. Pat wanted to call her Brenda and Mamma wanted to call her Maria. So they called her Brenda Maria. Somehow her birth certificate read Maria Bambina. I wrote this poem for her 57th birthday:

To baby Mary number 10

The day you were born – I remember when

I ran out the door – because I couldn't bear

The pain and suffering from our mother in there

Our grandmother brought you into this world

Guided by Mamma, whose strength was superb

And when you were born and all was calm

Our baby sister lay there and shone

57 years ago and lo and behold

Maria Bambina is still in our fold.

* * *

In 1939, Ruth Lowe had written, "I'll Never Smile Again" after the death of her first husband. It was first heard on C.B.C. Radio played by Percy Faith. She sent a copy of her song to one of the musicians she knew in the Tommy Dorsey band, hoping that Tommy would see it, which he did and agreed that it had merit. He arranged to have a very young, unknown singer named Frank Sinatra sing her song at the Canadian National Exhibition in 1940. It was a huge success. The teenagers went crazy over him. That launched Frank Sinatra's career, and Ruth Lowe's fame as the writer of that beautiful song. I was eleven years old, and who would imagine at that time that I would actually get to meet Ruth Lowe in person? In the 1950s I worked at the Club One Two, which was owned by her husband Nat Sandler along with Tommy Holmes and Lou Chesler.

The Club One Two was a beautiful nightclub, where you dressed to the nines and dined and danced to our house band, "Johnny Niosi", and you were there for the whole evening. It was very popular with the stockbrokers from Bay Street, and the lawyers and judges, the movers and shakers, and wannabe wise guys and high-class hookers. We also had a beautiful lounge, where the very talented Bill Butler entertained our guests on the piano. Also appearing was the equally talented Norm Amadeo, who in his 80s still entertained at various venues around town. You just can't keep good talent down.

I loved living on Claremont Street. We had a lot of fun playing outside, because there were a lot of children on our street. Almost everybody had a large family. Between our house and the next four adjoining houses, there were 42 kids. We had ten in our family. The Quaranto family had seven. Next to them the Deciano family had only four kids; this was considered a very small family. The Antonacci family had ten children and next door to them the Lofranco family had eleven. Just down the road a bit, the Loreti family had thirteen kids. And around the corner on Dundas Street, the Bagnato family had thirteen as well. Think about it: 68 kids from seven families!

Our streets were filled with people of various ages, from babies and toddlers to children and teenagers and adults young and old. I could go on and on with other large families on Bellwoods, Manning, Treford, Mansfield, Henderson and Grace, and we all pretty much knew everybody. Our neighbourhood was a hub of activity. We were all sisters and brothers. The road was our playground. We spent hours playing Red Rover, Kick the Can, and Hide and Seek.

Sometimes when I could go out to play, I had to take at least one or two of my little sisters and keep an eye on them. I hated this because I wanted to play Hide and Seek or Tag and not worry about them, so I would sit them on our front lawn or the sidewalk and warn them not to move from there *or else*. We didn't have to worry about cars because there were very few.

We didn't have toys to speak of. We made our own, like cutting out pictures of models from the Eaton's catalogue, and then cutting out the clothes to make our own paper dolls. We'd spend hours looking through the catalogue at all of the wonderful things that we couldn't buy, but all the same dreaming that someday we might. We played Jacks and Pick-Up-Sticks and Hopscotch and Double Dutch. We enjoyed playing the alphabet game while bouncing an Indian rubber ball. We'd start with the letter "A" and work our way through the alphabet. For example, "My name is Alice and my husband's name is Andrew and we came from Alaska and we peddled Apples." We had to swing our leg over the bouncing ball every time we mentioned the "A" word. You had to be pretty quick with the words. If you faltered you were out, and the next person starts, and so on. Our world was outside and we made our own fun. While walking along on the sidewalk we would chant, "Step on a crack, break your mother's back."

The young boys were busy doing their own thing, like making scooters out of old roller skates. My brother Ernie and his friend Frankie Bassano created their own telecommunication system, which they learned from instructions they got at the radio classes at the Columbus Boys Club. Frankie lived across the road from us, above Demacio's grocery store. He strung a wire from his window to our window in the third-floor front attic. They each attached a tin can to the wire and they were able to communicate.

We had great fun chasing after the ice wagon to grab a piece of ice to suck on. We had no refrigerators in those days, only iceboxes. We also had great fun chasing after the "Sheeny Man" with his horse and wagon. He wore a long black coat and a black top hat, and he had a long beard. He would holler, "Rags and bones," and we would run after him and mimic him. To us it was great fun, and I don't think he minded.

Living on Claremont Street was a non-stop event. There was always something going on in our neighbourhood. You really didn't have to plan your day. All you had to do was sit on your veranda and before long you would have a group of friends who were just walking by. There were church processions on the various saint days. I remember Susie and Santina, two very pretty girls, representing the Blessed Virgin Mary, dressed in the blue and white garb of Our Lady, carrying the banners. Thanks to Carmela and Fred Borsella, who organized these popular events.

There were also trips to the shrine at Mary Lake. The buses would be lined up on our street. The women, with their lunches packed and ready to board the buses, would be chasing the little children to get them on the bus. Even if you were not going on the trip, it was exciting to see all the action.

Occasionally we would have a street dance; our whole block on Claremont would be closed from Treford Place to Mansfield. The Antonacci brothers, who all played musical instruments, would sit on their veranda and play, and everybody danced, young and old alike.

Several of the Antonacci boys became professional musicians. Phil went on to become an accomplished saxophone player and performed with Tony Bennett and Henry Mancini, to name just two. In the 1940s he played with Bert Niosi at the Palais Royale Dance Hall. Sometimes he played at our church hall (St. Agnes) for our Sunday night dances. Phil had many opportunities to join legendary jazz musicians, but he turned them all down to be with his family, and besides, he couldn't give up his passion for hunting and fishing. Louis Antonacci played the accordion at Mastro's Restaurant on Wilson Avenue until his passing in his eighty-eighth year. Gino moved to California and played the piano for some of the stars, including Frank Sinatra. Sammy, Gregory and Willie also played at St. Agnes Hall on Sunday night. Sometimes they would all get on the back of a flatbed truck along with their friend "Boom Boom" Decino, who played the drums, and drive slowly all around the neighbourhood. Also playing for our Sunday night dances was Frank Busseri and his band. Frank's son is one of the Four Lads.

Sometimes the younger kids blocked Treford Place from Claremont to Bellwoods for a street dance. One time a Toronto newspaper sent a photographer to take pictures of all the action and it was in the newspaper the following morning. The principal at our school saw it and noticed that one of the girls was wearing pants. He thought it was Anne Marie Miele and summoned her to the office; he reprimanded her and said it was shameful for a girl to wear pants. Anne Marie tried to defend herself, saying that it wasn't her, because her father would not allow her to wear pants. Anne Marie had to bring her mother into the office before the principal would believe her.

Yes, it was a busy street. Everybody rode their bicycles up and down the street and some of the boys rode their homemade scooters or roller-skated. I didn't have roller skates, but my girlfriend, Jeana Deciano, sometimes loaned me hers. One day my Uncle Mario bought me a pair of roller skates. I was absolutely ecstatic, until Mamma told him to bring them back and get me a pair of shoes instead. I was mortified, but my uncle said, "No way I'm bringing them back, she deserves them!"

My uncle and grandparents lived across from us on Claremont Street. Sometimes Eleanor and I used to help my grandmother with some housework, and other times we would help make the homemade pasta. Imagine working the pasta dough around a long thin wire and then gently removing the wire. You would have long pasta with a hole in the middle. Making it was an all-day affair.

I loved my Nonna, but boy was she ever strict, more so than my mother. If she saw me playing outside with my friends, she would come over and tell the kids to go home and tell me to go inside to help Mamma. Of course I would be hopping mad and my mother would say to Nonna, "Ma, lascia sta (leave her alone), I told her to go out and play." I could understand her concern for Mamma; after all she was her daughter and having all of those children was a chore and a half. As far back as I can remember, my Nonna was at our house almost every day. She was always trying to help — and there was always so much to do. She often took the smaller children out to give her daughter a break. I especially enjoyed when she took us to the Orange Day parade on Queen Street and Strachan Avenue. The highlight of the parade was when King Billy came riding on his horse and my Nonna would say, "Oh, mo vene edu cu il cavallo!" in her Sicilian dialect, ("Oh, here comes the man on his horse!"). I find that very funny now. My grandmother was a devout Catholic and probably didn't even know what the parade was all about. (It commemorates the victory of Britain's Protestant King William over Ireland's Catholic King James II in 1690.) To her it was just another parade, and it was free.

As much as I loved my grandmother, sometimes we got tired of her "old fashioned" views. Every time we wore lipstick, she used to say, "God gave you red lips, you don't need lipstick." Or if we plucked our eyebrows, it was the same thing. When we did our laundry in the old wringer washers, she would say, "In Canada you have all the comforts. In Italy we had to take our laundry down to the sea and scrub them against the rocks," and so on and so on. Sometimes the rebel in me kicked in and I used to purposely sit beside her and put my lipstick on. But I still loved her.

Another special time was going to the Canadian National Exhibition. The school gave us tickets for Children's Day and Mamma would make fried green pepper and egg sandwiches, dandelion sandwiches and tomato sandwiches – made, of course, with fresh tomatoes from our garden. We would walk down to the C.N.E. at lunchtime and find a nice shady spot. Mamma always brought a tablecloth to lay down on the grass for the food, but my mind was on the hamburgers and onions sizzling nearby. My mouth was watering for them. Today I wouldn't trade a fried green pepper and egg sandwich for a hamburger, no way.

* * *

My grandfather was also always trying to help my mother. He would take the streetcar up to Hogg's Hollow with his shotgun and a burlap sack on his back to hunt for rabbits and groundhogs. He used to take my brother Joe with him, but after a few times, Joe refused to go. Between the smell of the animals and the smell of the Marco Gallo stogies (cigars) coming back on the streetcar, it made him sick, and it was embarrassing. We used to watch my grandfather skin the animals and then my mother would cook them. They were delicious, being the excellent cook that she was, but you had to be careful when you were eating because some of the pellets might still be in the meat. We didn't mind because we didn't get to eat meat all that much, except on Sunday. Sometimes during the week, she would make a stew with a little meat and a lot of vegetables and potatoes – or spareribs with cabbage and potatoes. (Spareribs were not expensive back then.) We got our protein from other foods, such as *pasta e fagioli*, the *fagioli* being lentils, chickpeas or peas, as opposed to Romano, navy or kidney beans. Being from Sicily, I guess she inherited the eclectic flavours, as Sicily was taken over by many cultures, each of which left their influence. When Mamma made the pasta with lentils we would invite our next-door neighbour, Helen Quaranto, to join us, as she absolutely loved the lentils.

Mamma never ran out of ideas on how to cook pasta. We had pasta with the aforementioned *fagioli*, or with broccoli, cauliflower, rapini, dandelion greens, eggplant, artichoke, ricotta, or fresh green fava beans. With the *fagioli*, she always used the short, cut pasta – either *tubettini* or *ditali*. With the ricotta, it was usually spaghettini, and when she cooked fresh green fava beans she always made the homemade pasta long and wide, like *pappardelle*.

We always had a big bag of flour, a sack of potatoes, cornmeal for the polenta, and lots of eggs. Mamma always bought the "cracks" because they were cheaper. Having these in your house was like having a security blanket and you could make wonderful pasta and gnocchi, etc.

One time in the spring, my parents bought a live lamb and we kept it in the cellar. We played with it until Easter time came. My grandfather was going to kill it for Easter dinner, which was why they bought it in the first place. Can you imagine the trauma us kids went through? We were sitting on the top stairs of the cellar crying and begging him not to kill the lamb, but of course he did. I cannot remember whether we were made to eat it or not, or maybe I don't want to remember.

* * *

I attended St. Francis of Assisi Catholic School, and my best memory was preparing for the St. Patrick's Day play. We rehearsed practically all year for this. Most of the teachers were Irish. It was exciting being in the play even though I had a small part doing the Irish Jig with a group of dancers. The plum parts were played by Annette Pitchot and Eddie Bagnato. They were the prince and princess. And Eddie and Eleanor Palladini got to sing, "Underneath the Spreading Chestnut Tree", a part I really wanted. It was fun dressing up in Irish costumes. The play was shown in the St. Francis Church hall. We performed in the afternoon for the students and in the evening for the parents and neighbours and friends. It was the highlight of our school year, and we have to thank Miss Harris for that. She was our gymnasium teacher. She taught us to dance the waltz, ballroom, the minuet, the Irish Jig, the Highland Fling, and the Sailor's Hornpipe. Tap dancing class was a breather from the other academic classes. For the most part I enjoyed school, but some things I didn't agree with, like having to attend Sunday Mass at nine o'clock. We were given little tickets by a teacher from school, and we had to hand them in to our teacher on Monday morning. It didn't matter that you attended mass at ten or eleven o'clock. It had to be nine o'clock, or you would be reprimanded. When I graduated from grade eight, I stopped going to mass on Sunday, because it seemed to me at that time that it was just another school subject that I didn't have to do. Now I realize that was a poor excuse.

There were a lot of things that were not right at school (by today's standards), like the strap we used to get for practically no reason, like chewing gum, or whispering to a classmate. One day in Miss Lundy's class (she was our music teacher), I drew a picture of a little girl and a little boy kissing, and wrote my friend's name and the name of the boy she liked. I was sitting towards the back and my friend was sitting in the front. I folded the picture several times and threw it along the floor to my friend. The teacher saw it and retrieved it before my friend could get it. She unfolded it and looked at me with a disgusted look on her face and ordered me up to the front of the class. She took out her strap and I knew I was in for a good one. Miss Lundy and Mr. Cassels were the two teachers who strapped the hardest. When she raised her hand I started to giggle and when she brought her hand down I pulled my hand away and she wound up strapping her lap. Her face turned red and she was so angry that I got a really good one that day. My hand was red and swollen. When I got home after school I wouldn't dare tell my mother that I got the strap, because she would probably give me more. In those days the teacher was always right, and that's the way it was.

I had to come home after school to help with the housework or care for the younger children. The only time I didn't have to come right home after regular school hours was to attend Italian lessons in a portable in our school yard. We were taught by this sweet little teacher with her hair pulled back in a bun and no bigger than a minute. Her name was Angelina Iannantuoni. There was also this very tall handsome Italian teacher. We named them "Mutt and Jeff" after the comic strip characters because of their different heights.

One day I decided to play hooky from Italian lessons and play baseball with my friends. Little did I know what was to happen. I was the catcher and when the batter, Helen, hit the ball, she threw the bat behind her and started to run to first base. I was looking at the ball and didn't see the bat coming toward me. It happened so fast. The bat hit me across the mouth and next thing I knew I was spitting out teeth. My mouth was bleeding and it started to swell, but I was afraid to go home because I was supposed to be in Italian class. News travels fast and my brother Lou came and brought me home. Mamma took one look at me and almost flipped. Next day, she brought me down to the dentist's office to Dr. Peter Andrachuk. My three front teeth were broken in half and the dentist pulled them out. If that had happened today, they would have been capped. Back then, who could have afforded caps? He told Mamma it would cost $25 for a partial plate. That was a lot of money for Mamma to pay so she went to see Helen's mother and asked her if she could pay half. She was a gracious lady and she consented, but she said, "Don't tell my husband."

Imagine going to school with three front teeth missing, and at the same time, because I had eczema, I had to wear calamine lotion on my face. Tony DeLuca, Patty Tanzola and Wilfred Pasquale (who later became my best man) used to tease the hell out of me. They used to say, "Hey Rosie, smile for us," and of course I would giggle, with my hand covering my mouth. I didn't giggle because I was happy. I think it was more a nervous reaction, because even when I was getting strapped by the teacher or spanked by my parents, I giggled. Thank God I didn't let things like that bother me too much.

Another day when I came home from school for lunch, I was rushing through because my friends and I were going to play Jacks, but my mother had other plans for me: she handed me a dust mop and told me to dust the bedrooms upstairs. Well needless to say, I was very angry and I started to argue, but one look from Mamma told me I had better keep quiet. I took the mop and stomped upstairs and when I reached the front bedroom I literally threw the mop from sheer frustration and it broke a window. Well I thought my life was over. I raced across the hall to the bathroom and locked the door before my mother got there. She tried unsuccessfully to open the door and when I thought she might break it down I took my chances; I was halfway out of the bathroom window, then I realized she'd quieted down. I said to her, "Why do I have to do everything around here? Why can't Eleanor do some work?" Of course I was around eleven years old at the time, so Eleanor would have been only eight years old. Anyhow, my mother quietly asked me to open the door and promised she wouldn't give me any "lickins", which she didn't. I guess with a large family and a big house, she had to count on Pat and me. In larger families, the responsibilities of childrearing and housework fell on the older females. Some of the girls in our neighbourhood got married just to get out of the house and away from all the responsibilities involved in a large family.

* * *

321454

Il presente passaporto consta di venti pagine

N. del Passaporto   N. del Registro corrispondente

382   1

IN NOME DI SUA MAESTÀ

VITTORIO EMANUELE III

PER GRAZIA DI DIO E PER VOLONTÀ DELLA NAZIONE

RE D'ITALIA

Passaporto

rilasciato a _Aliano Giuseppa_
Antonia

figlio di _Giuseppe_

e di _Barone Antonia_

nato a _Vita_

il _1889_

residente a _Vita_

in provincia di _Trapani_

di condizione _casalinga_

My mother's and grandfather's passports

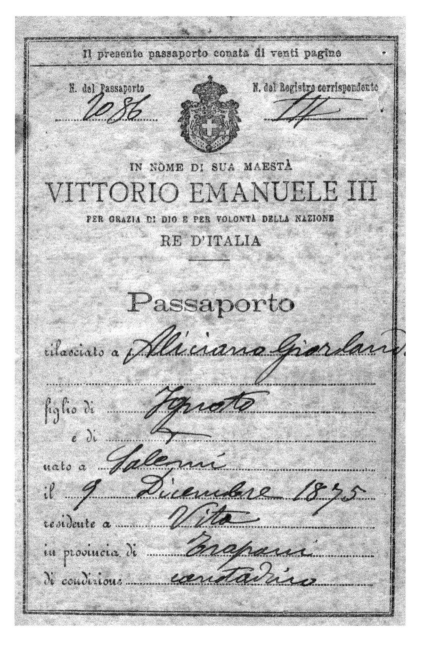

Opposite page: My grandfather, Luigi Vertolli, and my Aunt Glorindia with baby Domenic, my cousin

My parents' wedding picture: Riccardo and Giuseppa (Josephine) Vertolli were married at St. Agnes Church on October 11, 1920

Above: My father's brothers, from left to right: Fred, Emmanuel, Marcello, Arthur and Ernest

Right: Eustachio and Angelina Grieco with their three sons, Victor (my husband-to-be), Paul and Joseph

Mamma with my brother Ernie and baby sister Eleanor at our house at 502 Manning Avenue

My sister Pat, Mamma, baby Eleanor, and my brother Luciano ("Slim") at 502 Manning

Left to right: Eleanor, me, Pat and Joe

From top, clockwise: Luciano ("Slim"), Pat, me and Eleanor

Opposite page, top: Pat, Mamma and me visiting relatives in Hagersville, Ontario

Opposite page, bottom left: My dear grandmother, Antonia Giorlando, with baby Mary, Pat and Mamma, in the back yard of our home at 260 Claremont Street

Opposite page, bottom right: Mamma paid 25 cents for this picture of my sisters Gloria (standing) and Mary

* * *

During our summer holidays in 1939, when I was eleven years old, my brother Ernie and I, my girlfriends next door (Mary and Clara Quaranto) and Ralph Trauzzi, all got a job at a bakery on Dundas Street. We worked seven days a week for five dollars. We started at five p.m. and we had to work till we finished rolling a big batch of dough into buns. One time there was a new movie playing at the Centre Theatre, which was across the street from the bakery. It was "The Cat and the Canary", a remake of the 1927 silent movie. It starred Paulette Goddard, Bob Hope, and the mysterious Gale Sondergaard, who usually starred in spooky movies. We really wanted to see it, but the problem was we were all broke, because all our earnings went to our parents.

One day after the store was closed, someone knocked at the door. My brother Ernie opened the door and told him that the store was closed, but the man insisted that he really needed some bread, so Ernie sold it to him. So now, what to do with the money? The owners had left and the only other person was this guy who was there every night cleaning around and doing stuff, and he was always half tanked and smelled of booze. We all decided to keep the money and try to go to the later show. The other problem was, would we finish rolling the dough balls in time? Well, we worked like little beavers to try and finish, and when we were about three quarters done, we realized we wouldn't finish on time, so we dumped the rest of the dough behind some old equipment and went to see the movie. We really enjoyed the show. I don't know what happened to the dough; maybe that guy saw what we did and chucked it, because there was never any mention of it. Thinking about it now, I'm not proud of what we did, but at that time it seemed the right thing to do.

Another time during our summer holidays, we heard that they needed part-time help at Reliable Toy Co. on Carlaw Avenue. Some of us girls in the neighbourhood told our mothers about it and they gave us carfare and a lunch in case we were hired. What we did was walk to Carlaw Avenue and save the carfare money so we could spend it on ourselves. We didn't get hired. You see, in those days you did not go to your parents to ask for a nickel or a dime. You wouldn't get it anyways! When I think of some of the things the kids did for a nickel, it was downright funny. There was a store on College near Clinton that was like a confectionary store. They had a pinball machine and they sold pop and cigarettes, etc. And it was owned by "Sammy the Jew". (This was not being anti-Semitic, because everybody had a nickname.) The young boys used to go around to the back of his store and steal some of his empty pop bottles to sell back to him for a few pennies. At least they spent it in his store. And sometimes they would take a few pennies and cover them with silver paper and press on them till they indented them enough to look like nickels. Sometimes they got away with it.

One year, during a municipal election, the word was out that the Roebuck committee room on College Street was looking for kids to cheer for Mr. Roebuck and they would be paid a nickel. A bunch of us kids went up there and we cheered our little lungs out for that nickel. After all, a nickel could buy you a lot of candy. It was especially exciting to open a grab bag that we bought for a penny at Joe Bell's store on Mansfield Avenue. We often wondered how he could make a living selling a few candies. We realized later on, the real action was going on in the back room. Usually there were guys hanging around in front of Joe Bell's. They used to play "coins against the wall". My sister Mary and some of her friends stuck chewing gum under their shoes and waited for a chance to run in front of Joe Bell's hoping some coins would stick on their shoes. How many times we looked in every sewer to see if there were any coins down there, and if so, we would stick gum on the tip of a stick to try to pick them up.

Another time, a neighbour that lived across the street from us, Esther, asked my mother if I could take care of her two small children, as she was not well, and she would pay me. Of course this would go to my mother. Every dollar helped towards surviving. As young as we were, we didn't expect to keep any of our earnings. It didn't do us any harm, and I believe you should let your children know when a certain crisis occurs in the home, whether it be illness or financial trouble.

It makes a difference how you explain it to them. You should tell them in an optimistic way that things are not great now, but they will get better, instead of in a doom and gloom way. Your children have to know that life has many ups and downs and that you have to deal with them. I believe it will make them stronger and able to face life later on. If you try to protect them from "whatever", then I believe it will be harder for them to accept "whatever". Through all my life, no matter what life threw at me, I always felt that it was temporary and that things would get better. At no time did I ever give up hope, and that's always been my motto: If you give up hope, then you will get old before your time.

I was getting very frustrated caring for Esther's two children, because for one thing I could not reprimand them as I would my own siblings, or give them a little tap on the bum if I thought they were going to hurt themselves. In my family we were reprimanded not only from our parents but from our grandparents and our uncle and our older siblings. Anyhow, after about two weeks, I didn't have to care for them anymore and Esther gave my mother two dollars for my time.

* * *

There were a lot of horse-drawn wagons in those days. We had a horse trough at the southwest corner of Clinton and College. On the roadside there was water for the horses and on the sidewalk there was a drinking tap for the people. When the horses dropped their droppings (which we called horse-balls) the neighbours would run with their little shovels and scoop them up to use as fertilizer for their gardens. We used to bet on which neighbour would get there first. In winter, the guys used to use the frozen horse-balls as their hockey pucks.

And then there was the knife sharpener, who walked up and down the street with his grinder, ringing his bell to let the people know he was there. We also had the "Chicken Man", Mr. Vito Mezzapelli, who used to walk out on the road with a crate on wheels that was full of live chickens. If you wanted to have him kill and feather the chicken, he would charge you a few pennies more; he would take it home and his wife and children all helped in doing the work.

I remember my mother reaching into the crate and feeling for the one with a full breast and always buying the chickens with the brown feathers. She said they were better. You always heard people say, "Your mother made the best chicken soup." Sure they made the best soup, because they started out with a live chicken. How much fresher could it be? They used every part of the chicken except the toenails and beaks. They even used the intestines. My mother used to cut through them and soak them in salt water several times, then rinse them, and then she would tie them in a knot and drop them into the soup. We actually used to fight over them, and the giblets. My mother always ate the neck and the feet; she said she liked them best. When I think about it now, I know she just wanted to make sure there was enough chicken for the rest of us.

A while back, when my children were small, my husband won a turkey that was not dressed. I proceeded to cut the turkey and clean out the insides and cut through the giblets and remove all the guck. All the while, my children were watching in amazement – they thought I was Einstein. I mean, they only ever saw a chicken in the supermarket, all cleaned and plastic-wrapped.

There were others who came around selling their wares. The fish man with the fish on ice hollering, "Pesci freschi!" ("Fresh fish!") Your bread and milk were delivered every morning to your door. Then there were the fruit and vegetable peddlers who came in their horse-drawn wagons and hollered out their wares. The women would come out and look at all their produce and then the bargaining would start. Listening to them haggling back and forth to save a few pennies was a lesson in negotiating and/or economics. Mrs. Napolitano made ricotta in her home and went door to door to sell it. She was known as "la ricottara". There was a man with a camera and a pony who walked up and down our street asking if he could take a photograph of your child sitting on the pony, and he would charge twenty-five cents. They were all survivors trying to stay off the relief system.

These were the sounds of the city, the sounds of our neighbourhood, the sounds I miss the most. I also miss the aroma that filled the whole neighbourhood in the early fall season when everybody made their homemade wine and preserved tomatoes and made tomato paste. When my mother made the tomato paste, she spread the tomatoes out on a wooden board to dry in the sun, and us kids had to take turns shooing the flies away.

My mother really knew how to stretch a dollar. Many times she would send me to "Dempster's Staff of Life" on Dundas near Ossington, for day-old bread for just pennies. And how many times would our bread delivery man, Zio Nino Merlocco (he was my mother's *paesan* and related through marriage), leave us extra bread, saying he had bread left over, and my mother would say, "Sa benedica," in her Sicilian dialect. And who could forget those delicious "Charles Yeast Donuts", on Manning south of Dundas – five cents a dozen for day-old donuts.

As I said before, Mamma was a survivor. She made her own laundry soap. The grocery store across the street from us gave us all the fat from the sides of beef. She saved some of this fat to fry our French fries in. There was always a "chip pot" on the stove with this fat and it made delicious fries. She would then render the rest of the fat and pour it into a galvanized tub to make soap. She would pour lye into it and stir it. She'd let it solidify and then cut it into bars and store them in the cellar. We used this soap for our laundry and also to wash our hair. When we rinsed our hair, we used a little vinegar to make it shine. I mean, times were really tough! The storekeeper saved all the tissue paper that the oranges and lemons were individually wrapped in, and gave them to us to use for toilet tissue. We even used newspaper, cutting it into squares and piling them up. My mother would say, "Rub the papers together and that will soften them." (Years later, when my brother Joe was diagnosed with colon cancer, he joked about getting the cancer from wiping his bum with the newspaper with all the colon marks.)

Even though all of our parents were in the same situation, trying to survive as best they could, there were some families that seemed to be a notch above. Most of the men worked in construction and some worked in factories. The men who were streetcar conductors, mailmen and construction foremen were considered to have more prestigious jobs. We even considered the children of the local grocery stores luckier than us. But as children we played together and grew up together and it didn't matter to us. It wasn't until I got older that I realized that things could be better. But through it all, my mother, being the "Rock of Gibraltar", made sure we didn't go hungry. There was always food on the table (be it ever so humble) and there was never a doom and gloom atmosphere in our home.

* * *

I had the best of both culinary worlds – Sicilian cuisine from Mamma and the cuisine of the Abruzzi region from Pa. Mamma's *babbaluci* (snails) cooked in a light tomato sauce with lots of garlic. *Pasta e fagioli* with lentils and chickpeas. St. Joseph's Day celebrations that we looked forward to every March 19th. The wonderful *cucidati* (fig cookies) that she made every Christmas. And *sfinge* (deep-fried dough). Mamma was great at making Italian cookies but wasn't big on pies. From Pa's home town there was the *pasta all' amatriciana*, polenta, potato gnocchi, homemade liver sausage with grated orange rind, and crepes sprinkled with Romano cheese, rolled up, sliced, and dropped in hot chicken broth. On Shrove Tuesday, stacks of crepes layered with sauce and Romano cheese. At Easter time, the wonderful Easter pie was made with ricotta, salami, prosciutto and various other Italian cold cuts. It was extremely rich and delicious.

When we had polenta for supper, it was my father's job to cook the polenta because it required a lot of stirring – especially with a large family, when you had to use a really large pot. It was almost like a culinary ceremony. Mamma's job was to slowly add the cornmeal into the boiling water a little at a time to prevent lumping. During this time Pa would say to Mamma, "Piano, piano." ("Slowly, slowly.") When the polenta was cooked, Pa poured it onto our kitchen table, which had an enamel top; he'd spread the polenta with a big spatula and let it settle.

When Mamma made the tomato sauce for polenta, she always used the homemade cured Italian sausage that we called *salsiccia duro* (hard sausage). It had a distinctive taste and doesn't compare to the pepperoni used today. The name pepperoni was unheard of at that time. Mamma would cover the polenta with sauce, cut it into squares, and sprinkle Romano cheese on it. Then she made sure that each square had a slice of the sausage on it. After watching all this, with our mouths watering, we would sit down to eat. There were no dishes involved. We knew the drill. We had to take a square of polenta and pull it towards ourselves and eat it, then another and another, until you would see the polenta slowly disappearing off the table. Because I love polenta, I have learned along the way that you don't have to stir it for 25 minutes or so. You stir at the beginning slowly, a little at a time, until you incorporate all the polenta and make sure there are no lumps. Then you lower the heat and cover it. During the next 25 minutes you stir occasionally and cover it each time. It's easier on the arms. When the polenta is cooked, I like to add a little butter and some Romano cheese. It really snaps up the flavour.

Can you imagine what it was like around our dinner table, the twelve of us and whoever else happened to drop in? It was like having company that never left. Trying to keep ten children quiet at the table was a real chore. I was the target because I was the giggler. My brother Lou would make faces at me and I would giggle. Pa would tell me to stop, but I couldn't. I would try, but the minute I looked at Lou, he was ready for me and made more faces at me, and I would giggle more. Pa would get so angry and threaten to whack me, and then Mamma would get after Lou to stop.

* * *

There were ten grocery stores within a block. At that time supermarkets didn't exist. Eventually their opening led to the demise of the local corner grocery stores, many of which later were renovated and converted into homes.

There was Cappuccitti's on the corner of Claremont and Treford, Chiappetta's on the corner of Bellwoods and Treford, and Frediani's at Claremont and Mansfield (the last one to go). Demacio's store, across the street from us on Claremont, changed hands a few times. Mr. Longo took it over, then Mr. Giamatello, and then it went on to the DeFilippo family. On Mansfield, there was the Facchini family's store. At Mansfield and Clinton, there was Riccio family's, which later became (Frank) Formosa's. On Manning Avenue, there was the Marinangeli family and the Sebastiano family, and on Dundas, the Durbano family and the Giardine family.

Think about it, all within two minutes of each other. And it didn't matter which store you shopped in, you would know all of the customers and get caught up on all of the gossip. You only shopped for the day, and it was almost like a social gathering. You had to wait for your groceries; nothing was prepackaged. Everything was weighed in front of you – sugar, salt, pastas, etc. The fresh meats, as well as the cold cuts, were cut in front of you. Oh how well I remember going to Cappuccitti's, Frediani's and Demacio's to buy food and saying, "Put it on my mother's bill." They would immediately take out their journal and thumb through the worn pages to get to the "Vertolli" page to mark down our purchases. I sometimes wonder what we would have done if the grocery stores in our neighbourhood hadn't given us credit.

All of the grocery stores in our neighbourhood were Italian, and all of the dry goods stores, clothing stores and retail stores on College and Dundas were Jewish. Many times I went with my mother to shop. I remember at Mursky's Dry Goods store on Dundas Street, the bargaining that occurred over just a few pennies. But a sale was always made; they understood each other's need for survival in tough economic times.

I don't ever remember my father calling a plumber or an

electrician. He did everything himself. When he fixed the plugs on the toaster or the iron, he made us watch so we could learn to do it ourselves. We used to watch him fix our shoes. He had a shoe form, and with a sharp curved knife he would cut the leather to sole our shoes. It was no big deal; everybody did the same thing in our neighbourhood.

You didn't call anybody unless it was absolutely necessary – even the doctor. In those days you didn't have health coverage, so you didn't call him unless you really had to. My mother had her own home remedies. If you had a cold, she would make a mustard plaster and put it on your chest and back. If you burned yourself, she grated a potato and applied it to the burnt area. My grandfather also had his own remedies. If he cut himself, he poured bleach on the wound to kill any infection. If he felt his blood pressure up, he put leeches on his arm to suck the blood. He also boiled pomegranate skins and used the juice for toothaches and also to rinse his mouth to tighten his gums.

* * *

My mother started her day with the same routine. She would put on a cotton dress and then an apron over it. She combed her hair and tied it in a bun and pinned it at the nape of her neck. (This was before she became Canadianized and had it cut short and permed.) Now she was ready for the day, because you never knew who was going to drop in. In those days, friends didn't call ahead (not everybody had a phone) – they just came by. I especially remember when my great uncle, Zio Peppe Barone, came calling. It was always the same: he would knock on the door and come right in and say, "Wa-a-ay. Che permesso?" and immediately the coffee pot went on.

Everybody had a different way of calling. Some used to say, "Andoniella, are you home?" or, "Andoniella, che fai?" And my Aunt Grace, who was English, used to say, "Hello Maude, can I come in?" I cannot imagine where they came up with the name "Maude". Aunt Grace's children called her Aunt Maude. Those of my father's *paesans* who married English wives also called her Maude. My mother's name was Josephine. Nobody ever called her Josephine. Her brother Mario called her "Auntie". The neighbours and her Campotosto friends called her Andoniella, and her Sicilian *paesans* called her Doniccia. My father called her "Uaglio". You go figure.

In the evening it was always the same routine. Every night before my parents went to bed, Mamma would get a glass of water and put it on the night table, and a bed pan to put under the bed. During the winter months, Pa's routine was to check coal in the furnace. First he would sift through the ashes and save any coals that were not completely burnt. Then he would bed down the furnace, adding a few more coals so we could have a little heat during the night.

We didn't have hot running water, just cold. When we needed to take a bath, we had to go down the cellar and light the gas jacket heater to get our hot water. Things sure have changed. All you have to do today to get heat in your house is to turn up the thermostat. Now we are so spoiled, we flip if the TV remote doesn't work and we have to get off our butts to change the channel.

With my father, it was the same every morning. Shaving with the straight razor at the kitchen sink with his shaving strap hanging on a nail nearby, which was very handy for him when he needed to grab it to whack us when we did something "bad". When our parents spanked us, it wasn't because we did anything really bad. Sure, it was to discipline us, but mostly it was from sheer frustration on their part – hard times, lean years. The same situation today would have warranted a few words of warning, not to do it again. I mean, they didn't beat us or anything like that. We learned early on in life the art of self-defence. We bobbed and weaved and we really didn't get hurt all that much.

The events of Sunday morning at our house usually began Saturday night. We had to polish our shoes (the only pair we had) so they would look good for Sunday Mass. Saturday, Mamma would buy a live chicken from the "Chicken Man", Mr. Mezzapelli, and by the evening it was in the soup pot. She would snap its neck and hang it upside down so that the blood would drain into the head. She then plucked the feathers and singed the remaining little feathers. Our kitchen smelled like a barnyard. When the soup was ready, because we had no refrigeration, she would bring the big pot down to the cellar and leave it on the cold concrete floor with cold water running under it. Sunday morning was usually chaotic getting everybody up for mass. Mamma always had a problem getting my older brothers up.

In our neighbourhood, as was likely the case in most Italian neighbourhoods, on any given Sunday morning, across the whole neighbourhood you could smell the meatballs frying and the *sugo* (tomato sauce) simmering. When Mamma fried the meatballs, she warned us not to touch them, as she counted each and every one of them. Can you imagine if we'd all sneaked one (because they were so hard to resist)? There would have been very few left to put in the *sugo*. There is nothing tastier than a fried meatball.

Sunday dinner was always chicken soup made with *pastina* and sometimes with tiny meatballs added. We also had macaroni and meatballs. It didn't matter which pasta you bought – it was all called macaroni. When Mamma made the homemade pasta, she called it *tagliatelle,* and for the soup it was *tagliolini,* which was thinner. Sometimes she would cut the long strips of *tagliatelle* into little squares, which were called *quadrucci,* also for soup. Sunday dinner was always served at one o'clock and was our main meal of the day (a tradition carried on in many Italian homes today). The evening meal was usually leftovers and/ or cold cuts, olives, and always a salad and celery sticks with salt and pepper and a small bowl of extra virgin olive oil for dipping. Sometimes when Mamma made *sugo* during the week, she would add spareribs or homemade Italian sausage or neck bones, pig's tails or pork hock. I like to add spareribs to my *sugo* because it gives it a really nice flavour, and also Italian sausage. As for the neck bones and pig's tails, which I like, they're a hard sell for my children and grandchildren.

* * *

Christmastime at our house was always festive, regardless of how tough it was economically. Uncle Mario always helped at this time of year. He bought us our Christmas tree and he helped in buying the food for the traditional fish dishes on Christmas Eve. He also bought the alcohol to make liqueurs. I loved watching Mamma make all the colourful liqueurs, like creme de menthe, anisette, strega and rosolio. She looked like a mad scientist at work, although she herself never touched a drop of alcohol in her entire life.

It was economical to buy the alcohol and make your own. She did this because at Christmastime, friends would drop in and it was customary to offer them a liqueur and biscotti. I guess it was just the festive season that made us feel good. It wasn't as though we received any presents or anything, which was okay because we didn't expect any. What we did wait for were the Star Boxes that were given to all the poor children in the neighbourhood from the Star Fresh Air Fund and distributed by the Columbus Boys Club during the late 30s and early 40s. Boy, how we waited for that. One year they were late in delivering them. Here it was Christmas morning and no Star Boxes. We literally had our noses pressed against the front window hoping and waiting, until finally we saw a car stop in front of our house and we all screeched with delight when they walked up to our door. We put them all under the tree. Thank goodness our names were on the boxes; this way we wouldn't have to fight over them. Each box contained a pair of stockings that were so itchy that we scratched all the time we wore them. We got mittens and a sweater, a box of candies and a game, either Snakes and Ladders, checkers or a jigsaw puzzle. Whatever it was, it made us very happy, and having a box of candies of your very own was really something.

Usually everything was given to us in little pieces. Sometimes my father would bring home a "Sweet Marie" chocolate bar and slice it into several pieces and give us each a taste. One day Pa brought home a basket of cherries and said to Mamma, "Wash these and let the kids eat as much as they want." And sometimes my Nonna would bring a *fico d'India* (prickly pear) and we'd watch her expertly peel it without pricking herself with the needles. (It sure was named right!) Then she'd slice it and give a piece to each of us. On Christmas Eve, we hung up our stockings and we almost always could predict what was in them — an apple, an orange, and a few walnuts. These were all special treats for us. I guess it was all the other things Mamma did that made Christmastime enjoyable, like baking all the biscotti two weeks before and hiding them. On Christmas Eve we all got to stay up late, and the whole family, including my grandparents and my uncle, sat around the dining room table and played *Tombola* (like Bingo) while Mamma was in the kitchen cooking all of the fish dishes and frying *sfinge*. She would be humming away and enjoying every bit of it. As midnight approached, the older ones went to Midnight Mass. Outside, the streets were alive with people also going to mass and shouting greetings to one another.

On New Year's Eve, it was pretty much the same. At midnight we all went out on the veranda and beat pots and pans together and shouted greetings to everybody, because they were all out doing the same thing. One year, Mamma was not home; she was in the hospital. It had started a couple of days after Christmas. At that time my Uncle Marcello from Kirkland Lake was visiting us. She began to hemorrhage and we took her to Western Hospital. On New Year's Eve she was still in hospital, and that day I went to see her. She looked so pale I cried all the way home. New Year's Eve without Mamma at home was very depressing. My grandparents and uncle were there as always, and my sister Pat, who was like our second mother, took charge. At that time I didn't quite understand what was wrong with Mamma because nobody said anything. Later on Pat told me that she had miscarried. I believe that was when the doctors decided that she had had enough; after eleven births and a few miscarriages they made sure she couldn't get pregnant again.

I wrote this poem in 1975 for my parents' 55th wedding anniversary, which we celebrated at the Beverly Hills Hotel on Wilson Avenue:

Friends and family old and new

I have a little story to tell all of you

It happened many years ago – it happened here in town

Two people came from Italy – from separate little towns

They met here in Toronto – they didn't waste much time

To tie the knot – to say "I do"

But holy gee if they only knew

Well first came Louie in '21 – Luciano (Slim) was born in '23

Pasqualina (Pat) in '24 – bear in mind there were no T.V.'s

Ernie was born in '26 – I came along in '28

Eleanor was born in '31 – golly gee think of all the fun

Joe appeared in '33 – Joanie was born in '36

Gloria made it in '38 – you'd think by now they'd close that gate

But no such thing – there was no stoppin'

And lo and behold – little Mary came a poppin'

Well enough is enough I always say – if it keeps up, who's going to pay?

We think they had enough fun in the hay

The Doctor agreed – so we had her spayed

Well, there were good times and there were bad

There were hard times and there were glad

There were times when we wanted to run and hide

But with their love – we all survived

55 years ago started all the fuss

And the proof is right here with the 52 of us

Almost one a year – those odds aren't bad

And this is the story of our Mom and Dad!

* * *

All through the Depression and the lean years, they never gave up their traditions. Christmastime with the cooking of the fish on Christmas Eve. In better times there was calamari, *babbaluci*, smelts, baccala, etc. In leaner years, even if we had one fish dish and spaghettini with anchovies, it was just fine.

Another great tradition was preparing for the St. Joseph's Day dinner, on March 19th. Mamma made a sauce with tomato, fennel, sardines and raisins, and served it over spaghettini topped with lightly toasted bread crumbs seasoned with a little crushed fennel seed and a pinch of sugar. The seasoning mix for this sauce is available today in most Italian markets under the brand name "Cuoco". Grated cheese is absolutely forbidden on this. When I make this pasta at home, my children want to sneak some cheese and I say to them, "If Grandma were here, she'd whack you one!" She also made stuffed artichoke. And of course the *zeppole* – stuffed puff pastry filled with custard or sweetened ricotta or whipped cream with a cherry on top. Today you can buy them at most Italian bakeries.

Sometimes on St. Joseph's Day we would be invited out for a special dinner by some of Mamma's Sicilian *paesans*. I especially enjoyed when Zia Rosa Ferlito invited us. She lived on a farm in Scarborough. She would have a huge nativity scene in her home made up of evergreen branches with apples and oranges hanging from them. From her guests she would pick someone to represent Jesus, Mary and Joseph. When dinner was ready, they were the first to go to the table and everyone else would follow. It was quite a celebration. Another time we were invited to Sanci's Deli on Danforth Avenue to celebrate St. Joseph's Day. The Sanci family lived upstairs from the deli. This is a wonderful tradition to keep up, which I still do, and my children and grandchildren look forward to it, although I don't go as far as doing a nativity scene.

* * *

I graduated from grade eight at the age of twelve. When my teacher asked me what high school I decided on, I told her I wasn't able to go because my mother needed me at home to take care of the children, because she was going to go to work. The teacher told the principal and the principal sent for my mother and told her that she was doing the wrong thing by keeping me away from high school and that it was not fair for me, as I was a bright child and should have the opportunity of an education. My mother, in her broken English, said, "I am sorry, but I must work and she must take care of the children." My older sister Pat, who was sixteen years old at the time, was lucky enough to have found a job. She couldn't afford to have Pat stay home, so I was next in line.

During the war years, when Italy entered the war on the side of the Germans, it was very difficult for Italians in Canada to get work. All of a sudden hundreds of Italian men were rounded up and interned, some of them for as long as three years.

James Franceschini had come from Italy with nothing at the age of fifteen. Like many Italian immigrants he started working in construction and worked his way up, creating a huge construction and building supply company, and was able to keep a lot of people employed. One day in 1940, the RCMP came into his office and took him away, and then sold off most of his assets. There were many others like him, like Julius Molinaro, who were interned. There was never any proof that we were ever a threat to Canada. After all the discrimination the Italians had faced in the early years in Canada, after living and working in this country and finally believing that we were accepted, we were once again discriminated against without cause. Ironically, during World War Two, Julius Molinaro aided the Allied Forces' Office of War Information in Northern Africa and Italy, and later he became a professor at the University of Toronto. And James Franceschini, being the resourceful person that he was, started up his business again and wound up building the Queen Elizabeth highway.

And I remember our friend and neighbour Antoinette Bassano (Toni Ciccarelli) – how humiliated she was when the RCMP went to her workplace at the post office, took her away, fingerprinted her, and said she was an enemy alien. Many were fingerprinted and photographed and ordered to report monthly to the RCMP. Many were interned – hardworking and decent people being herded into camps and treated like common criminals, while many of their sons were fighting for Canada, some of whom were killed in action.

Places like the Casa d'Italia consulate on Beverley Street were taken over by the RCMP. Believe me, it was not a good time for the Italians. One thing that was for sure: you could always count on the Jewish people to hire you. They knew what discrimination was all about. As a child, I remember, down at Crowes Beach and other beaches, signs that read "No Jews Allowed", "No Jews Or Dogs Allowed" and "Gentiles Only". As kids we were used to seeing these signs. When I tell my children this, they find it hard to believe that our government actually allowed this. As I said before, the Jewish people hired the Italians, and if someone got a job, they would in turn tell their friends and try to get them jobs as well. My sister Pat got a job at the Belt Manufacturing Company on the Esplanade through our cousin Mary, and pretty soon a bunch of friends from our neighbourhood got jobs there. Sam Nobleman was the foreman, as was his brother Joe, who later opened his own business in diamonds. It was here that lifelong friendships blossomed between Pat and the Noblemans and some of the neighbourhood girls.

Being young, I didn't realize the seriousness of war; after all, the war was *over there*. We had news on the radio with Jim Hunter every night at six o'clock, and the newspaper, and the News of the Week at the theatres, but we didn't have the day-to-day TV news to show us the horrors of the war. I remember my parents having concerns, and my grandfather, who every time the news mentioned bad things about Mussolini would say, "Bulla shita" in his broken English. It's because when he still lived in Italy, in his eyes Mussolini had been a good leader, and maybe he had been back then, but Mamma was afraid that my grandfather would also be interned. The thought of my brothers going to war weighed heavily on her. As it turned out, my brother Lou had chronic bronchitis and was rejected, as was my brother Slim. My brother Ernie, who wanted to join the Air Force and even lied about his age, was also rejected because of something to do with his eyes.

But we knew it was serious when we started hearing the air raid sirens and we had to turn all our lights out. The whole city was blacked out. If you had an emergency in your house, you had to cover your window with a blanket in case of an air attack. There were air raid wardens on every block to make sure that you did. During the times of the blackouts, my sister Pat would take the small children and sit beside them on the bed and reassure them that everything was okay. I remember Pat always making things out to be better than they really were. One Christmas Eve, she actually had the small children believing that they heard Santa and his reindeer on the roof.

On December 7th, 1941, the Japanese bombed Pearl Harbor and the United States entered the war. In February 1942, Japanese Canadians were sent to internment camps in British Columbia. Also in 1942 came the rationing of tea, coffee, sugar, and then gasoline. Depending on the number of people in your family, you were given ration coupons that you had to give to the store when you bought your goods. (The food rationing did not end until November, 1947.) In the summer of 1942 came the news that the C.N.E. (Canadian National Exhibition) would remain closed for the duration of the war. Almost immediately, the C.N.E. buildings were taken over by the army, navy and air force. They did mock attacks at Sunnyside. The sight of jeeps and tanks and military trucks downtown made you realize that the threat of war could very well be here, and every time a plane flew over us, we wondered if they were the enemy, and we would be afraid that they were going to drop a bomb on us. Wars, the scourge of the universe!

* * *

It was tough taking care of the house, the cleaning, the cooking, and taking care of the younger children. Mary was one year old, Gloria was three, Joanie was five, Joe was seven. I really had my hands full! (Eleanor was nine and in school all day.) I would get up early in the morning and start the coal stove in the kitchen, and when it was warm I would get the children up. Then I would start my chores. Before my mother went to work she would tell me what to make for supper, but sometimes, she would say, "Arrangia." ("Make do.") Make do with what?

Some days were really frustrating, especially when I hadn't a clue what to make. In the summer it was easier. We had a small garden in our back yard, and we had tomatoes, vegetables and herbs, etc. I would pick tomatoes, green beans, zucchini, onions, and with a lot of potatoes I would make a big pot of stew. I had to make enough for the twelve of us. Sometimes when the stew was almost ready, in order to add some protein I would crack a dozen or so whole eggs, one at a time, and drop them in the stew. When the eggs cooked, it was ready. When my mother dished out the stew, she made sure that we all got one egg and it was great dipping our crusty Italian bread in it. It was around this time that "Lipton's Chicken Noodle Soup" was introduced. It was great because with three or four packages of soup I could make enough for all of us. I would start by adding escarole, a type of endive, to the boiling water, add extra *capellini* pasta, and then the soup mixture. When it was ready I would then beat six or seven eggs with some Romano cheese and add them to the soup. I guess you could call it *stracciatella* soup.

My favourite summertime meal, and the easiest to make, was the *perciatelli* pasta with uncooked fresh garden tomatoes. It works okay with canned tomatoes, but it doesn't compare to the fresh. All I had to do was chop the tomatoes and a lot of fresh basil and parsley, then add lots of minced garlic, salt and pepper, and extra virgin olive oil. I would prepare this ahead of time in a large bowl and then all I had to do at suppertime was cook the pasta, drain it, and add it to the sauce. The heat of the pasta brought out all the flavours and the aroma filled the whole kitchen. Everybody loved this, and of course with every meal we had a salad and lots of crusty Italian bread.

One day, on my mother's birthday, my grandmother came over

(she was always at our house trying to help me) and she said she was going to make a cake for her. While I was busy doing things around the house, she made the cake. But something was terribly wrong. I asked her what she used to make the cake with and she showed me a brown bag that she thought was flour. It was a bag of plaster that my father had used the day before to patch something and hadn't put it back in its place. Needless to say the cake wound up in the garbage. My grandmother felt so bad, and I went upstairs to my bedroom and cried because we wasted eggs and milk and especially the sugar (because we were allowed only so much per family). In all their years in Canada, my grandparents never learned how to read or speak English. If my grandmother had, she would have been able to read the writing on the plaster bag.

Always when my grandparents came over to our house (which was practically every day), my father would have a sarcastic remark like, "Here they are again!" or, "Can't they stay home?" And one day when he wasn't in the best of moods, he actually told them to go home, and escorted them out the door. I was so upset that I went upstairs to my bedroom (my bedroom, my "Shangri-La") and cried. When my mother came home from work, I told her what happened and asked her, "Why would he do something like that?" That's when she told me the story about the man on the ship that they had wanted her to marry instead of my father. So all through the years, they more or less tolerated each other. I mean he wasn't mean to them or anything like that. And sometimes they actually seemed to be enjoying each other's company. Anyhow, the next day they were back as though nothing happened, and life went on as usual.

When my grandmother passed away in 1949, I was devastated, and when my father showed some remorse at her passing it made me feel better. I didn't want to think that he actually disliked her. Sometimes you don't appreciate things till you lose them. Sometimes I wonder if my grandparents ever thought of what it would have been like if my mother had married the man on the boat. Perhaps her life would have been easier, maybe not as many children – who knows? But I'm glad she married my father, or I wouldn't be here writing this story.

* * *

I felt so sorry for my mother. Sometimes after the children were in bed, she would stay up late sewing and mending and patching the children's clothes. She made our underpants from bleached sugar bags. We wore designer label underwear, the more popular brand being "Redpath". She also made our dresses from material given to her when we were on relief, so Pat, Eleanor and I all got to wear the same dresses. (Oh Joy!) She worked very hard, but still when I think about it now, she accepted her role in life. She used to sing a lot while she was cooking or puttering around in the kitchen and she was always smiling. Once in a while she would sing this song and it seemed as though she was reminiscing while she was singing. One day I asked her where she learned that song, as it was not one of the usual songs she sang. (Her favourite was "Santa Lucia".) She said that back in Sicily a young boy used to sing it to her, but tragically he'd fallen into a well and drowned.

I know my mother felt bad for me having to do everything while she worked, but did she really have a choice? Putting food on the table was the number one priority. Some of our relatives and even some of the neighbours thought that I was too young to have all this responsibility, but I really didn't mind. Or, to put it another way, there were no choices; you just did it.

* * *

In 1942, when I turned fourteen years old, my mother took me to an office on Bond Street to get a work permit to work full-time. I took her job at the clothing factory and she stayed home. I thought I'd died and gone to heaven.

I worked at the corner of Markham and College at Superior Men's Tailoring. We made men's pants in our department and right next to us they made soldier's uniforms. My Uncle Mario had been the foreman but was called up to the army. Our new foreman was Al

Luftspring, a great guy with a wonderful sense of humour, and we had a lot of fun. I worked with a great bunch of people: my friend Caroline Tanti, my Mamma's *paesan* Zia Rosa Ferlito, Mary Schwartz, Alice Gauthier, Maxie, Landau, Chidlowski, Ginsberg, Rubinoff. It was amazing how we were able to talk back and forth over the noise of the machines. Once in a while the big bosses, Mr. Ritchie and Mr. Farber, would come around. Mr. Ritchie was the more serious one, while Mr. Farber was the more flamboyant one. Mr. Ritchie's son Jack worked there, and I thought what a really nice guy he was, despite being the boss's son – really down to earth.

In those days we worked from eight a.m. to six p.m. and half days on Saturday. I was on piecework. My job was bushelling – clipping threads on the finished product, men's pants. I later graduated to being a special machines operator – tacking, buttons, buttonhole and looper. My first pay was $20.97 and we were paid cash in little brown envelopes. I could hardly wait to bring this pay home to my Mamma. Out of my whole week's pay she gave me twenty-five cents to go to the show.

A lot of people in our neighbourhood worked beside us in the uniforms department. My cousin Molly worked there; Frankie, the brother of my friend Lena Tanti, also worked there and I developed a huge crush on him. There was a snack bar on the lower level run by Mr. and Mrs. Ginsberg, and all the employees in the uniform department had to walk by our machines to get to the door leading downstairs. When Frankie walked by he would gesture with his head as if to say, are you coming? I would immediately leave my machine and join him. Would you believe this was the moment I looked forward to every day? Ah, young love! Sometimes we would meet at my house on a Saturday morning with some friends and go down to the Sunnyside swimming pool, which we called the Tank, and sometimes we would go for a walk in the park holding hands. That was the extent of our relationship. He never made a move on me, never even tried to kiss me. He was a real gentleman. (Darn!) Of course we were only about fourteen years old.

Another of my Mamma's *paesans*, Dorothy Lotto, worked there along with her two sidekicks Ollie and Elsie (the Three Musketeers). Boy, what a lively trio they were, always laughing and kibitzing. It was a pleasure to be in their company. At Christmastime Elsie gave me a present. It was an "Evening in Paris" gift box. I had never received a real Christmas present before. Any gifts we received were from the Star Boxes. Sometimes my sister Pat would make little homemade gifts for the small children. Getting a real gift, especially cologne and dusting powder at the age of fourteen, was very impressive.

Because I was the youngest person working there, it seemed everybody was protective of me, especially the people I knew from the neighbourhood. Albert "Chellagher" Micelli used to say to me, "Watch the wise guys," or words to that effect. The presser Mr. Ginsberg (whose hands shook so much it was amazing how he was able to do his work), bought me a Pepsi almost every day. Zia Rosa Ferlito gave me a piece of fruit at lunchtime every day. One day on her lunch hour she went out to College Street to buy some *babbaluci* and left them by the window. It rained that day and the snails got out of the bag and began to crawl all over the windows. It sure was a funny sight to see everybody trying to grab the snails and put them back in the bag.

I enjoyed my job there, even though I had to hand in my whole pay at home. When I was 15 years old my mother took me to Rose's Dress Shop on College Street and bought me a green wool suit for Easter. You can't imagine how I felt wearing a brand new suit. On Easter Sunday a lot of the girls wore custom-made suits and "Tammy Taft" hats and they would go walking down the boardwalk at Sunnyside, which on Easter Sunday was a must.

It was around this time that I began to experience a shortness of breath. I couldn't climb the stairs without stopping to rest. I could not keep up with my work, so they hired someone to help me. Being on piecework, my pay was cut in half. I went to the doctor and he said I had a heart murmur and not to worry about it and try to take it easy – I should grow out of it. I felt so guilty that my pay was less. Walking home from work I used to think, wouldn't it be nice if I found some money to bring home, wouldn't it be nice if Mamma had a nice roast for supper, wouldn't it be nice, if-if-if-if...

When I started to feel better and was able to do my work and get more pay, I mustered up enough courage to ask Mamma if I could just pay her room and board. She looked at me for a moment and I thought, "*Oh, God*, did I just commit a mortal sin?" And then she said, "Si Rosa, é giusta." ("That's fair.") When I told Pat what happened, she said to me, "See Rose, I told you, you should have asked sooner." (At what point growing up does it change, from being the child, spanked and disciplined, to having the camaraderie that sets in between parent and child and becoming best friends?)

So now I was able to keep two dollars out of my pay. I felt quite independent. Out of this money I was able to clothe myself. I was a saver. If I needed to buy a dress or a suit, I would go to Rose's Dress Shop and put one dollar down and pay one dollar a week until it was paid for. And oh how I guarded my clothes. Eleanor used to sneak some of my clothes and put them back before I got home from work. I always knew when she did this. I would get upset and let her know it, because I wanted to keep what few outfits I had in good condition. Anyhow as we got a little older, my sisters could borrow anything from me. Being frugal helped us to survive. At that time there was the "Toni Home Perm" kit, and my friend and I would give each other a permanent at home. I also gave my siblings perms and we all saved money.

Buying things "on time" was a part of life then. There was a Mr. Mozart who used to come to our homes with a couple of suitcases filled with *biancheria* (sheets, pillowcases and tablecloths). Once, my mother bought two sets of sheets and pillowcases with Madeira work, and she paid him twenty-five cents a week. They were for Pat and I to put in our trousseaus.

She also made tea towels out of bleached sugar bags and then pressed on transfers so we could embroider them and put them in our trousseaus. As times were still not great, my mother had some work brought to our home. These were crepe dress-fronts that had to be beaded and sequined. She taught my sisters Pat and Eleanor and me how to do them. Sometimes even my brother Lou would help. We would all sit at the dining room table after supper and work on them.

Mamma also did cooking at Italian weddings on weekends. In those years you rented a church hall and you hired cooks. Mrs. Spadacini had a regular crew that she called to help her with the cooking and preparing. As well as my mother there was Ethel Magnacca, Annie DiFlorio, Sis Pillo, Kay Sabatino and others. There was no such thing as "so much per head". You invited the whole family, kids and all. It was an all-day affair. The couple got married in the morning and went to the photo studio for pictures. Then it was off to the hall for lunch (usually family, *comares* and *compares*). At night, there would be a big dinner and reception for everybody. At around eleven o'clock the bride and groom would leave to go home and change into their "going away" suits and then come back to the reception. (Choosing the going away suit was almost as important as choosing the wedding gown.) They would stay for a short while and then say their good-byes and then off on their honeymoon.

At the end of the night the cooks cleaned up and were able to take some of the food home – usually chicken, pizza and pasta. Not the pizza as we know it today; we had no pizzerias. Most of the Italian weddings ordered their party-size pizzas from Beaver Bread, formerly on Lightbourn Avenue. The topping consisted of just tomato sauce, Romano cheese and oregano. The leftover food was sent to Scott's Mission.

* * *

The war ended in 1945, and when we got the news at the factory everybody cheered. Some of the women who worked there had sons and husbands overseas, in active duty. They got up on the cutting tables and danced and everybody hugged each other. I will never forget that day. We left work and I ran all the way home, and already the streets were filling up with people. Boy, what a party we had on Clinton Street in front of the Monarch Hotel and next door at Beefy's kibby joint (where San Francesco Foods is today). Beefy played the ukulele, my brother Lou played the guitar, Sammy Tambrano played the banjo, and the Antonacci brothers all played their instruments, and the whole neighbourhood was there. What a time we had. We danced and jitterbugged and did the conga line up and down Clinton Street. They burned a Hitler effigy, which was hanging from a tree in front of Bitondo's store. To keep the fire going, some of the guys sent little Angela Spizzeri to get more wood from the fences at Grace Street Public School.

But there was also sadness for some of the families in our neighbourhood. Johnny Depinto, who was only 19 years old, and lived right across the street from us, was killed; Nunzio "Nuncy" Leone, who lived on Manning Avenue, was in the Air Force, and he too was killed; Buddy Bagnato was injured and was paralyzed from the waist down and spent the rest of his life in a wheelchair.

* * *

Above: Exchanging coats and hats with servicemen. Photo taken on the Crawford Street bridge. Front row left to right: Pat Vertolli, Mary Rosano, Antoinette Bassano, Anne Rosano.

Left: Mary Rosano, Pat Vertolli, Antoinette Bassano with two servicemen on the Crawford Street bridge

Opposite page: A Navy officer (name unknown) with my sister Pat's friend Tim (right) on deck during World Two

July 16/44

H.Q. 7 C.V.A
B.W.E.F.
C.A.O.

Dear Patsy:

It's been a dogs age since I last heard from you & I guess it has been close to that since I wrote to you. Sorry dear. I've had it pretty tough since D-Day, so you will forgive me. (Of course.) Well thanks a lot anyw. How are you anyway Patsy I'm feeling pretty good these days. Lets hope until the war is over. I'll feel this good all the time. Of course, sometimes a guy gets real scared but it wears off. There has been plenty of times

Part of a letter written to my sister Pat' by her friend Tim on July 16th, 1944

that I have been scared
so bad that I could hardly
breath. Just about 15 times
as bad as seeing a
spooky film. But I guess
its just "Grin & bear it it."
Well I guess thats about
all I can tell you about
my self right now, so
lets change the subject
to you.
        How is things in
Toronto? You know its
going to be great to
see good old Toronto again
(if I ever do).
        How are things at the
club? Pretty busy with
a canteen, dances etc. I

Next page: Celebrating VE Day (Victory in Europe Day, May 8, 1945) in front of the Monarch Hotel and Beefy's kibby joint on Clinton Street

* * *

We were very fortunate to have jobs that were within walking distance. Upstairs in our building was Kimball Paper Products, and at Manning and College a whole lot of other friends worked at Nemo's Foundation, where they made brassieres and girdles. Upstairs was the famous Frank Buckley's Cough Syrup. Other friends worked in the garment district down on Spadina Avenue. We all saved on carfare.

Actually everything that we needed was within walking distance. We had a travel agency on the corner of Claremont and Mansfield, run by the Misuri family. Lobraico Insurance and Notary Public was at Manning and Mansfield. We had a post office on Bellwoods at Mansfield, run by Angelo Gabriele and Maria Luigina Grimaldi; Mr. Grimaldi was the first Italian postmaster in Toronto. The post office was later demolished to make way for the expansion of Grace Street Pulic School. We had two funeral parlours – Lobraico's on Dundas near Grace and Moffat's on College near Manning, where a few of the guys had once broken in and taken a stiff (a dead body). They put ice skates on him and, holding him up, skated all around the back lane, which had been flooded so that the kids would have a rink. Mischievous kids doing anything for a laugh...

We had four barber shops: DiStasi's on the corner of Henderson and Clinton; Sannuto's on College Street; Belvedere's on Dundas near Grace, and Matteo's on Mansfield Avenue. When Matteo wasn't busy, he would play his guitar and soon some of his friends who were hanging around would go home to get their accordions, and they would pass the time playing until a customer walked in. When our parish priest, Father Riccardo went for a haircut, he would say, "Why you no come to church? I give you *my* business." Matteo would reply, "I'm-a too busy." Father Riccardo would say, "You no too busy to go to the Monarch for a beer" or, "You no too busy to go hunting," and so on. Poor Matteo; the guys were always playing tricks on him. They always knew when he was loading his car with hunting gear; one time they hung around and when he and his son Louie went into the house to get more gear, they jacked up the back wheel. When Matteo was all packed and ready to go, the car wouldn't move. After much frustration and a few choice words they finally told him. Sometimes when he'd been away hunting, he would come home to find a big For Sale sign on his window. The same guys playing tricks. It's amazing how they still remained friends.

We had two Chinese laundries, one on the corner of Clinton and Gore, and Lee's Hand Laundry on Dundas and Bellwoods. There was a shoe repair shop on Clinton Street and Jaffe's clothing store at Mansfield and Manning. On Clinton Street below College was the St. Patrick Social Club, which was owned by Bertie Mignacco. It had a pool table and a pinball machine and everyone played cards; also there was often some horse-betting going on.

On College Street between Euclid and Montrose it was all retail stores and a variety of other businesses: Lipson's Egg and Honey, where some of the women in our neighbourhood, including my mother, worked part-time, cracking eggs and putting them in pails to be delivered to pastry shops. There was Appel Poultry. There were two fish markets, Cohen's and Grupstein's. Mr. Grupstein had three sons – Nat, Joe and Harry. Joe and Harry had a group called "Joe King and his Zaniaks" that played at various venues around town, including the famous Brown Derby on Yonge Street. The boys had a passion for the ponies and Mr. Grupstein used to say, with a smile on his face, "Oy, my boys have a sickness."

We had two drug stores, Greer's (which later became Rayburn's) and Sam Leiberman's. We also went to Frank's Drug Store on Dundas Street. Our neighbourhood cleaners was Cadet Cleaners, located where Bar Diplomatico is today. Before the Pylon Theatre was built, which is now The Royal, there was a market, which looked like an arcade; it had stalls on either side and a huge roller-skating rink in the back. We had the wonderful Health Bread Bakery, which had the best pastries around. There was Sam's Automotive, with a gas pump out front. There was Greaves Jam Company, Weinstock's Tailoring, Daniel's Shoe Store, Pylon Lunch, Bellman's Hardware Store (the last to go), Rose's Dress

Shop, Gotleib's Dry Goods, Satock's Dry Goods, and further along, at 714 College Street, Sam Sniderman started his record business and made it big. He was soon known as "Sam the Record Man". As teenagers, we used to go to his shop and listen to our favourite records in the listening booths. Sometimes we bought a record, if we had money, but Sam was a good guy; he probably knew that nine times out of ten we wouldn't be buying a record, but he never said anything.

We also had our fair share of doctors and dentists, from Bathurst Street to Ossington Avenue. Our doctors were Dr. Scandiffio, Dr. Andrachuk, Dr. Shwab, Dr. Albert Reingold, Dr. Cohen, Dr. Suchuk, Dr. Levine and, further along College Street at Spadina, was Dr. Isabella Wood, who delivered most of the babies in our neighbourhood. And going further back in time, there was Dr. Fontinella, who lived on Grace just below College, where the Johnny Lombardi family now resides. Our dentists were Dr. Burstein, Dr. Kay, Dr. Witchel and Dr. Andrachuk. These offices were all within walking distance.

We had it all, all within our own neighbourhood. Of all of these, the only business that is still there is the Bank of Montreal at College and Manning, the only reminder of what used to be.

* * *

St. Agnes Church was previously called St. Francis Church. It was established in 1902 and was run by the Salesian Fathers. Sunday Mass was said in the basement for the Italian parishioners. The priest at that time was Monsignor McCann. In 1914, as the Italian population increased, the church was given over to the Italian community of Toronto's west end. Monsignor McCann immediately went about acquiring a new St. Francis Church at Grace and Mansfield, which opened in 1918, and the church he left behind was re-named. In 1934 the Salesian Fathers left the parish in the hands of the Franciscan Fathers.

St. Agnes Church was a mecca for the Italian community, not only for our parents when they arrived but also for us, growing up in this tightly knit neighbourhood. They opened up their hearts and doors to the many traditions that the Italian immigrants brought over. St. Agnes Church offered something for every age group. They turned the basement into a boxing club for the young boys in our neighbourhood, until later when the Columbus Boys Club opened. The Columbus Boys Club and St. Agnes Church always worked together for the good of our youth. The basement was later turned into a men's recreation club for the Italian men. It offered a snack bar, soft drinks, and tables for card-playing and general socializing. Because of the fast-growing Italian population in the west end, the men's club was later converted into a chapel for use on Sunday.

During the 30s, 40s and 50s, St. Agnes Church offered a multitude of activities for our community. There was the Y.P.C. (Young People's Club), which held their first annual dance in 1937. They organized annual picnics at Exhibition Park. In the 40s we had the C.Y.O. (Catholic Youth Organization). We held meetings at the priest's house and had a dance every Friday night at the church hall for the younger teenagers; on Sunday nights there was a dance for the older youth. Frank Busseri played there with his band, as did the Antonacci brothers. During the war years, the hall was turned into a canteen for the servicemen. We had the St. Agnes Peewee Softball League, St. Agnes Bowling League, and the Canadian Italian Hockey League, which was founded by Louis Jannetta. There was also the Circolo Calabrese Society of St. Agnes, the St. Agnes Women's Auxiliary and the St. Lucy Society, which offered pilgrimages to the shrine of Sainte-Anne-de-Beaupré in Quebec and the Martyrs' Shrine in Midland, Ontario; every February they celebrated Mardi Gras in the church hall. The Italo-Canadese Society – which Joseph Bagnato founded and was its president – was also housed by the church. As I said before, St. Agnes Church was truly a mecca for our parents and subsequently for us.

And then there was "Amazing Grace" Bagnato, the matriarch of the Bagnato family. Because of her command of the English language, she was able to help many of our new Italian immigrants when they arrived. She would speak for them, help them in filling out forms or legal documents, etc. Many went to her for advice; being new in this country, they needed some guidance. She was also a court interpreter at City Hall. She was a going concern. Some of the immigrants she helped paid her back by doing some ironing, some household duties, etc. Lord knows she needed some help raising thirteen children. She truly was an Amazing Grace. There is a plaque in her honour at the corner of Mansfield and Grace.

There were others ready to give a helping hand to newcomers, including Mamma. When some of Pa's *paesans* came over from Campotosto and lived in a flat with just a hotplate to cook on, Mamma cooked their beans every day on our coal stove. She was always there to help with whatever. When Pa's brother, Uncle Rizziero, came over in the 50s with his daughter Luigina and son Renzo, they stayed with us until they could get a place of their own and send for the rest of their family. It was great fun having Luigina and Renzo around. They were pleasant and always smiling and it was instant camaraderie with our new first cousins. Simple acts like these meant a lot to newcomers, and helped them adapt to their new life here.

Mamma was happy to be able to help anyone who needed it, like Aunt Nora, who lived in Kirkland Lake. She had a friend whose son had a problem with his leg and had to come to Toronto to go to Sick Children's Hospital. Aunt Nora phoned Mamma and asked if she would help them when they arrived. They stayed with us and Mamma helped with the little boy's leg therapy. When my cousins Dom and Norman came to Toronto from Kirkland Lake they even brought a friend, and they all stayed with us. Mamma wouldn't have it any other way. When you have ten children, what's a few more?

Raising ten children in tough times took guts, sacrifice, perseverance and compromise. And I believe that dealing with the problems of life head-on with hope and optimism is the key to survival. But sometimes, no matter how strong you think you are, there are moments when your problems become too much, and there has to be an outlet. With Mamma, we always knew when she reached this point. She would become very quiet while she was doing her chores, and she would do them at a slower pace than usual. We would try to engage her in small talk and try to joke with her but she would not respond, which was out of character because usually she was a happy person. At this point we'd watch her very carefully, and sure enough she would drop whatever she had in her hand and start screaming. We'd hold onto her till she stopped and she'd always apologize and tell us not to worry, that she would be alright. And she always was, until the next time. Everybody has a different way of dealing with stress and I guess that was her way. Thinking about it now, it was a good thing that she could scream it out. Imagine keeping all that inside you; you would be a very good candidate for a nervous breakdown.

* * *

Most of the immigrants arrived here with little or no schooling, but the men knew about bricks and stone and building, and they didn't mind getting their hands dirty. I remember the men going to work, getting on a streetcar with a pick and a shovel. They learned a lot about sewer and drainage work. Some of them were able to start little jobs on their own. They'd buy a little pick-up truck and a wheelbarrow and some tools, and as their sons grew older, they worked together and learned the trade. From these humble beginnings, and because their families stuck together and made it work, they went on to start their own successful businesses. To name a few families from our own neighbourhood: the Collinis, Valentinis, Spadacinis, Ciampinis, Lofrancos, Reginas, Pocis, Cancellis, Dimos and Violas.

Some of these families went on to become millionaires. My father never had that goal. He had knowledge of building and construction, but he was quite content to come home from work and have supper and maybe a glass of wine and relax and play his *organetto*. Who knows? Maybe if he had been more business-minded, perhaps together with my older brothers they might have started something.

He might have been easygoing in some ways, but he sure was strict in other areas. When we were young, we all had to be seated at the dinner table before we could start eating. This is what I was used to. When my own children were little, I used to wait until my husband came home from work before we sat down to dinner. At that time he owned a dump truck and worked for contractors. Sometimes he didn't get home till seven or even later. He insisted that we have dinner and not wait for him. He was right; how insensitive it was on my part to make the children wait. It stemmed from my childhood – nobody got to eat until everybody was seated – and you ate whatever was put in front of you. No second choice. Oh, excuse me, we did have a choice: "Take it or leave it."

How different things are today, compared to when I was young. My parents never said, "I love you" but they showed it in the sacrifices they made to raise us properly. In a large family, the older siblings looked out for the younger ones. Today, parents are like chauffeurs: drive me here, drive me there, drive me to hockey practice, soccer practice – you're at your children's beck and call. Most children today are still in school past the age of twenty. In my day, twenty was pretty much the marrying age, and most of us had been in the workforce since we were fourteen. In most families, if the boys did not go to work, they were kicked out of the house. My brother Ernie was fifteen or sixteen years old when my father told him to get a job or get out. Ernie chose to leave and join the rest of the gang who were also kicked out.

Mind you, some of the boys chose to leave on their own, so as not to live under their parents' rule. They hung out at Trinity Bellwoods Park and used to sleep in the trucks in DiLeo's lumberyard, which was situated behind our back lane. I used to bring sandwiches to Ernie in the park. Sometimes, when they were in the lumberyard, Ernie and whoever was with him would come to our back door after my father went to work and my mother would make them breakfast. One time my father found out that I was bringing sandwiches to Ernie and blamed me for Ernie not working because I was feeding him.

What really bothered me was that my brother Louie did not work all that much either – so why wasn't he kicked out? There is something about the firstborn son, traditionally named after the paternal grandfather, that seemed to make him the favourite. Ernie was the more quiet type; Louie, on the other hand, was able to convince my father that he really was looking for work. One time, Louie went to the Columbus Boys Club and put plaster of Paris on his arm to make it look like a cast. He told my parents that he broke his arm, so that they wouldn't pester him about looking for a job. It was all I could do to keep my mouth shut and not squeal on him. Sometimes, when my parents weren't around, he would slide the cast off and start punching me and my sister Pat in the arm. He wasn't hurting us. He was just kibitzing around with the arm that was supposed to be broken. He thought that was very funny.

* * *

Every Saturday was housecleaning day. We had to scrub the hardwood floors with steel wool and then wax them with a paste wax, and when the wax dried we had to use a heavyweight brush and go back and forth on the floor to bring up the shine. Then we had to use a soft cloth under the brush and go back and forth once again to make it shine like glass. Believe me; you didn't need to join any fitness class. It was hard work but we were used to it. The only carpeting we had were the long runners in the hall and in the dining room leading to the kitchen, and these we took outside and swept. This was a ritual every Saturday morning. This wasn't so much a chore, it was actually enjoyable, because my girlfriends next door, Mary and Clara Quaranto, and next to them Jeana Deciano and Stella Lofranco, were all doing the same thing. We would be chatting back and forth and listening to the loud music coming from our houses' open windows. It's unthinkable that we could do our housework without music! We listened to a lot of "cowboy songs" in those days and songs of the "Hit Parade". Watching a tribute to Martin Scorsese on TV one night and listening to him talk about his mother and all the other Italian ladies in their neighbourhood, I couldn't believe the similarities between their lifestyle and my own. I guess "Little Italy" is the same no matter which city you live in.

If my friends and I had plans to do something that day, we would work really fast to finish our housework, and in no way did our plans come before our housework. I can just picture it, saying to my mother, "Ma, I can't clean the house today, because me and my friends have plans." Yeah, right! She would have clipped me good. Sometimes my friends and I helped each other so we could finish sooner. When I think of those days, I wonder why it was always the females in the family who did all the housework. I don't ever remember my brothers having to do any chores. Pat and I did most of the housework, and when Eleanor got older she was expected to help, too. I suppose if there were no females in the family, the boys might have had to do it.

One day after we had finished all the floors, my brothers started to drag their guitars and amplifiers back into the living room. I started to tell them not to drag their equipment, but to lift it instead, but their devious minds went into overdrive; they winked at each other and my brother Ernie started to flick ashes from his cigarette onto the floor. That sent me into an uncontrollable tantrum. I started screaming at them and went stomping upstairs to my bedroom and cried. My mother got after the guys to leave me alone, and my sister Pat came up to my bedroom and said, "Why do you let them get your goat? They're downstairs laughing and you're upstairs crying." One thing about our family – we never held grudges. We argued, we yelled, we voiced our opinions, but we never stayed mad for long.

We also had a lot of fun at home. We kibitzed and horsed around a lot. We had an old piano that someone gave us and everybody learned how to play it. My brothers Lou and Slim played the guitar and my father played the *organetto*. There was always music in our home. I especially enjoyed when Lou, Slim and Pat played together during the "Boogie Woogie" era. Their fingers would literally fly up and down the piano keys, and they would change places and start all over again. Did Mamma mind all the racket? Not at all! I really believe that music helped get us through the tough times.

We were never allowed to go out as often as we wanted to, but we could always bring our friends home. My sister Pat used to bring some friends home from work on a Saturday night. I would help her move the furniture to one side, and we would put on records and dance and jitterbug to the tunes of the Andrews Sisters, Glenn Miller, Artie Shaw, etc. And who could ever forget the morale-lifting songs of Vera Lynn during those awful war years. "The White Cliffs of Dover", "We'll Meet Again", "Yours", "Auf Wiedersehn Sweetheart" and "Lili Marlene". I am sure she must have helped win the war!

I loved it when Pat would bring a friend from work to stay overnight. One time she brought this girl named Hilda. She was a black girl staying at the YWCA, and going to medical school and working part-time; I often wondered if she became a doctor. Another time she brought home a girl named Tootsie. Boy, was she ever a ball of fire. My sister Pat and I shared a bed, so whoever stayed over had to sleep with us. Tootsie was a great storyteller and her off-colour jokes were something else. I used to pretend I was sleeping, otherwise Pat would tell Tootsie to watch her mouth, but I wanted to hear the stories, too. When Tootsie got married, Pat was her maid of honour, and they remained friends their whole lives.

There were others. I often wondered what happened to Betty McCrone and Mary Hunter. And one day Pat brought home this skinny little blonde Danish girl named Lillian Larsen. Pat said to our mother, "Ma, feed her, she looks like she's starving. She brings lettuce sandwiches to work." Well, that started a friendship that lasted a lifetime and continues over several generations. Over the years she spent many days and nights at our home. She was like our own sister. On Sunday nights, Pat and my brothers Lou and Slim would go to the dance at St. Agnes Church hall, and many times they took Lillian.

Sometimes some of Pat's friends would meet at our house before the dance and the conversations would go something like this; "Are my seams straight?" (Silk stocking with a seam down the back), "Is my slip showing?", "Can I borrow your sweater?" (No jeans in those days). One night my brothers and sister took me to the dance at Columbus Hall on Sherbourne Street. I was probably the youngest there. I was shy and was hoping nobody would ask me to dance. My brothers took turns dancing with me. I remember this guy they called "Seabiscuit". Seabiscuit was the name of a very famous racehorse and they really named this guy right. He literally raced around the dance floor at a very fast pace and everybody would get out of his way.

Usually when they got home after a dance, they wanted to snack. There was always a chip pot on the stove and they could make French fries any time, but sometimes they wanted something different. My father put a padlock on the icebox so they wouldn't raid it, not that there was a heck of a lot to choose from, but whatever was there was probably for next day's dinner. He also put a padlock on the cellar door, because we had preserves there that my parents used to make. My father used to make his own prosciutto and hard sausage and pickled pig's feet. My mother made pickled eggplant and peppers, and whatever else was cheaper or in season, to preserve for the winter. When my mother did her preserving, Pat and I had to help, but if we were menstruating at the time, we were not allowed to help for fear of spoiling the food. Sometimes we tried to trick her and say we couldn't help because it was the wrong time of the month. Yeah right; she was smarter than us!

On these nights when Pat had her friends come over, my mother would go visit her *comare* down the street, and my father would saunter over to the Monarch Hotel to have a few beers and socialize with friends. The history of the Monarch Hotel goes back to the turn of the century. According to John E. Zucchi's book, "Italians in Toronto", in the early 1900s Francesco Tomaiuolo opened up a private bank and steamship agency on the corner of Clinton and Henderson (the hotel's future site). He gained the trust of the new immigrants, who felt comfortable dealing with a *paesan*. The immigrants scrimped and saved whatever they could to be able to save enough money to buy a house – at that time, for $2,000 more or less. Everything seemed to be going well for him. He had many clients. When some of his clients came to withdraw their money to buy a house, there were no funds. He'd spent the money renovating his bank and had opened a small hotel, which he initially called the Venezia Hotel. He hadn't counted on the Great Depression to hit. Franceso Tomaiuolo went bankrupt and a lot of his clients lost their life savings.

The hotel was later owned by Roy Worters. He was a goalie, and all the hockey players and sports people used to go there. I remember as a kid, my father, my uncles, my grandfather and a lot of the men in the neighbourhood going there. It was the neighbourhood pub. It was a social gathering place. Everybody knew everybody. On the main floor it was "Men Only" and upstairs was a sign, "Ladies with Escorts". They also had rooms for rent upstairs, hence the name "Hotel".

When Mussolini decided to side with Hitler, all of a sudden the Italians became the enemy, a threat to our country. It was then that the name was changed to the Monarch Hotel. Roy Worters sold it to Frank Perelli and then it was sold to Paul Sitzer. Later generations of young people frequented the Monarch, but times had changed. In the old days only the men went there. Later on, everybody would go.

It was a very popular place to go to, especially when Peter Pesce worked there as the manager downstairs. I'm sure everybody came just to see the crazy antics he used to pull off. Even the television people came in a few times and filmed him and it was shown on TV. One day, one of his daily customers, Joey, came in and told Peter he had a toothache. His tooth was loose and he was afraid to go to the dentist. Peter told him to sit down and he would take care of it. Peter came out with a tray, a glass of beer, a pair of pliers and a white serviette on his arm. Joey rinsed his mouth with the beer and then drank it, and Peter pulled his tooth out; all the other customers applauded. The Monarch was a fun place to be. Paul Sitzer sponsored the Monarch Bowling League team and most of the guys on the team were from the neighbourhood, including my future husband.

Even though most of us moved away, when my sisters and I used to get together, we would always wind up in the old district and go to the Monarch for dinner, but mostly to kibitz with our friend Kenny Guggins, the bartender, who'd worked there for 35 years. But things changed and unfortunately the Monarch Hotel closed down. I never thought I would live to see that day. It was so much a part of our neighbourhood – a landmark! It was closed for two years and then re-opened, but it will never quite be the same as it was back then.

* * *

Then there were the "clubhouses", which were usually started by groups of friends. One club, "Club Kallie", started in August 1946; they celebrated their 50th Anniversary in 1996, and they still get together. The original members were: Peter Collini, Freddie Maddalena, Joe Chiappetta, Jimmy and Mike Pesce, Johnny LoFeodo, Mike DeBonis, Alfie Loreti, Vince Trauzzi, Johnny Dario, and Dave Antonacci. On their first anniversary, in 1947, they held a father and son banquet in the Pesce/Bush back yard.

There were other clubhouses where groups of friends got together. Some of these clubs were in the members' garages. Now *there's* a place I would love to have had a video camera. One time in Luigi Spadacini's clubhouse on Bellwoods, they brought some girls; when Mr. Spadacini was starting to walk towards the garage, the guys said, "Ix-nay, here comes the old man." The girls started to run out of the garage and in his broken English Mr. Spadacini said (so the story goes), "Hey bebe, no go, com-ma back." There were many clubs in those early years. There was Club 21, Club Marie, Club Perkyville, Club Bernard, and Club 12. There was also the Casino Girls Club.

There was always something for the boys to do, especially at the Columbus Boys Club, which was originally situated on Queen Street near Bellwoods. It was a storefront with a gymnasium on the second floor. In 1936, it moved to 123 Bellwoods Avenue. Words cannot express the influence the Club had on our youth. I cannot even imagine our neighbourhood without it.

The Club was founded by Hector MacNeil under the auspices
of the Knights of Columbus. He was recommended above a lot of other
candidates to be director of the "New Boys Club" when it opened up in
the fall of 1929. He was born in Nova Scotia and attended St. Francis
Xavier High School and College; he received his B.A. in 1924. He then
entered Notre Dame University on a Knights of Columbus scholarship
and successfully completed a program on Boys Leadership, receiving
his M.A., and a specialist diploma in Boys Guidance. In 1926, he was
engaged by the Knights of Columbus at Mount Vernon, New York,
to serve as organizer and director of their Boys Club Program; here he
developed a close relationship amongst the Italian-American boys of
that city. He was very sports-minded and a great athlete, having played
football and hockey for the varsity teams at St. Francis Xavier and also
coached hockey at Notre Dame. I would say the committee made an
excellent choice. Hector was the perfect person and a great role model
back then for our young boys. His motto was "the other fellow". He
purchased a house at 119 Howard Park Avenue and later moved to
Ossington Avenue, where he settled nicely into our neighbourhood with
his wife "Skip", as she was known, their three daughters, Neila, Moira
and Paula, and their two sons, Hector Junior and Bobby.

One year, when I was nine years old, the Club gave a Christmas
party at the Piccadilly Hotel and invited all the kids in the neighbourhood.
I remember it well because we had never attended anything like that
before. We had entertainment and a wonderful dinner. There was
a young kid on stage performing magic tricks. His name was Albert
Robertson (we called him Robbie). Meeting him was the beginning of
a lifelong friendship with our family. He grew up in Little Italy and
was greatly influenced by Hector MacNeil and another leader, Carmen
Bush. Robbie spent a lot of time at the club, where he got the chance
to learn the art of boxing. During the Second World War he enlisted in
the Royal Canadian Armoured Corps, and rose to the ranks of Sergeant;
he became the Canadian army boxing champion and later Canadian

featherweight champion.

Robbie always had a passion for doing magic tricks and spent many hours practicing; he became an accomplished magician known as "Kid Houdini", and performed at various functions. In those years he was good friends with Ronnie Hawkins, who gave Robbie's young nephew (Robbie Robertson, of "The Band" fame) his first gig.

Robbie was always looking for something more. He decided to join the Brotherhood at the Immaculate Conception Novitiate in Dundas, Ontario. After a while he left the novitiate; in 1964 he entered the Oblate Novitiate, and took his final vows in 1979.

Using his talent for magic and comedy, Brother Rob invented and perfected a character, "Tony Spagoni the Mad Magician", and performed weekly to audiences and at charity and fundraising functions year round. Returning to Toronto in 1991, he soon met up with his old buddy George Chuvalo, who also worked with troubled youths and drug addicts. Brother Rob – another product of the Columbus Boys Club.

The club was a haven for the boys. They especially looked forward to the Saturday night movies that were shown there, and to the annual Christmas parties with entertainers, like Robbie Robertson performing his magic tricks as "Fifi the Clown", with his outrageously colourful clothes. The children would ask him, "Where did you get your vest?"

And he'd answer, "From VEST Virginia."

"Where did you get your hat?"

"From ManHATten."

"Where did you get your pants?"

"From PANTSylvania."

"Where did you get your shoes?"

"SHOEcago."

And the children laughed and laughed at his corny but funny jokes. At the end of the evening, the kids were given some goodies to take home, which had been donated by businesses in the neighbourhood; the bags to put the goodies in were donated by Honest Ed's. The club offered all sorts of crafts and workshops – printing, radio, music, leatherwork, basket weaving, clay moulding, woodworking – and of course, boxing and all other sports.

Two men in particular, Carmen Bush and Pat Zona, volunteered their time to coach and help the kids in any way they could. After a few years of volunteer work, Carmen was hired as sports director. What he did for these boys was truly an act of dedication and selflessness.

All the parents had great respect for Hector and Carmen. They could always count on Hector if their boys got into a little trouble – nothing serious. One time my brother Lou and his friend "Spinach" stole some baskets from the fruit peddler's wagon, to sell for a few pennies. They were caught and taken to 311 Jarvis Street, a place for juvenile delinquents. Hector was called to help them. He went to speak on their behalf and to bring them home, but my mother said, "Keep my son overnight." Some of the other mothers thought she was being cruel, but my mother knew exactly what she was doing.

The parents were as grateful for the club as the boys were. It made up for the fact that many parents were too busy to spend time with their children – mothers with large families, fathers who worked on construction all day and went to bed early. Most of them never took their children fishing or to baseball games. There was never any time for this father and son stuff, but thanks to Carmen Bush, who had a passion for sports, the boys had organized leagues and played in Trinity Bellwoods Park. The young boys with dirty faces played with such a passion to win. You might remember some of the teams back then: the

Gorevale Rats, the Lizzies, the Mansfield Tigers, the Manning Sluggers. If you do, then "God Bless You".

Sometimes when Carmen needed to transport his football team to their games, he'd call on his old buddy Pat Zona, who owned a dump truck, and all the guys with their uniforms would pile on to the back of the truck. Pat was always there to help Carmen. They don't come any better. Carmen dedicated his whole life to sports. Today he is listed in Canada's Baseball Hall of Fame. The east baseball diamond in Talbot Park, at Bayview and Eglinton, is named the Bush-Hibbert Field, and at Richview Park, in Etobicoke, you will find the Carmen Bush Baseball Diamond.

As time went on, some of the older boys got together and formed the Columbus Club Old Boys Association, headed by Robbie Robertson, Vic Bagnato, Eddie Jackson, and Moose Muszinskie. They organized all kinds of functions, raising money for the club and for scholarships for the promising students of St. Francis of Assisi Catholic School. Some of the members organized the distribution of the "Star Boxes" donated by the Toronto Star Santa Claus Fund. One of the members, Sam Manna, started delivering the boxes to the various homes in 1948 – and sixty years later he was still helping out. He also helped at the Santa Claus Parade warehouse to organize the parade route. Sam, and many others who dedicated their time and effort to the club were a godsend for our youth. Most of the kids grew up to be responsible citizens; some of them strayed and had skirmishes with the law, but eventually their roots kicked in and they grew up.

There were many other young boys influenced by the club and by the MacNeil family, including my brothers Ernie ("Sleepy") and Joe. They were very involved with the club and also with the Columbus Boys Camp in Orillia.

Joe helped every summer at the camp – in the kitchen, washing floors, washing pots, and helping to cook. The ones doing this work were known as the kitchen rats. Finally at the age of eighteen, he started to get paid and worked every summer at the camp and every winter at the club, always under the guidance of Hector MacNeil. At age 25, Joe joined the Ontario Provincial Police force.

Sleepy worked as a janitor at the club and every summer at the camp. He then decided to enter the religious order of the Immaculate Conception Novitiate in Dundas, Ontario. After six months he became disenchanted with the cloistered life. He decided to go back to school to finish his high school diploma, which he did at St. Michael's. After one year, he skipped second and went on to third year because of his high marks. He completed his fourth year and then attended Ryerson Institute (now Ryerson University). After Ryerson, he went to the Huronia Regional Hospital, where he worked as a registered nursing assistant until his retirement.

There were many young boys whose training at the club influenced their future livelihood. My sister Pat donated her time teaching the kids leathercraft, which she'd learned when she worked at the Belt Manufacturing Company. Toots Papalia and Jimmy DePede were instructors in the printing class. They taught many kids the art of printing, which became their livelihood: to name a few, Leo Moynahan, who went on to work at the Toronto Star; Gordie Weinholdt, who had his own printing business, as did Joe Parro. Joe's brother started Tony Parro Carpentry.

Sadly, the Columbus Boys Club closed its doors on April 30, 1977. There were other clubs that helped our youths back then, including the Kiwanis Club, situated in Trinity Bellwoods Park, which was for boys and girls, and the Dovercourt Club at College and Dovercourt, now the West End YMCA.

* * *

In the old days, before TV, video games, and computers, we listened to the radio. It was great, because you could do your housework, your ironing, etc., and listen to your favourite radio shows at the same time.

We listened to great comedians like George Burns and Gracie Allen, Fibber McGee and Molly, and Jack Benny and his sidekick Rochester. Then there were the spooky shows like "Inner Sanctum", "The Shadow" and "The Creaking Door". When these shows were on, we turned out all the lights and you really thought you were part of the show. (I sometimes wonder, did we really need TV?)

There were a lot of things to do for the younger and older teenagers and those in their early twenties. There was dancing at the Palais Royale to the Jack Evans Orchestra, and at the Palace Pier to the Trump Davidson Band. There was dancing under the stars at the Seabreeze, down by the lake, and also at Biggards, where you saw some real fancy jitterbugging. We had the huge Sunnyside Amusement Park and swimming at the Sunnyside Tank, and who could forget Duggan's Hamburger for a red hot and a Vernor's ginger ale.

One time, my next-door neighbours had visitors from Guelph – Teresa and Carmel Timarchi. Mary and Clara Quaranto and I decided to take Teresa and Carmel to Sunnyside Amusement Park. It was always a lot of fun there. We walked around and went on rides, and when we were leaving the Ferris wheel, a couple of soldiers asked us to go on again and said they would pay. We were all for it except for Teresa – she didn't think it was proper – but we went on anyway. Keep in mind, these were war years and there were a lot of servicemen around. When we were ready to leave the park, some soldiers offered to drive us home. Again, Teresa thought we were really awful to accept the ride, but we did anyway; it was no big deal to hitch a ride and we all piled in. Teresa went back to Guelph and I didn't see her again until she moved to Toronto in 1946. She would become one of my closest and dearest friends for life.

One time Mary and I had a date with two soldiers, and they were picking us up at Mary's house. When Mr. Quaranto saw the uniforms, he invited them in and started to tell them of his experience in the Italian Army. He literally got on the floor and went through the motion of combat. We were totally embarrassed. We tried to get them out of there but they were actually enjoying themselves. Some girls really went for the uniform.

When the Quaranto family moved away from Claremont Street, I really missed them, but Mary and I kept in touch. She then met the handsome Nick Bruno, a young soldier just returning from active duty overseas. They eventually got married. The four of us had great times together, and spent a lot of time swimming in the Humber River. When our daughter Patricia was born, we asked Nick and Mary to be the godparents.

College Street was where the neighbourhood gathered. It was the focal point of all the happenings. Everybody walked up to College, although sometimes it took you an hour to get there, because you stopped to talk to your friends, who were sitting on their verandas. We generally just walked around, back and forth, stopping to talk to friends and just watching the guys horsing around. Sometimes they would do something mischievous, like letting the chickens out of their cages at the Appel Poultry store, and the chickens would be running all over College Street.

Another time, what started as fun turned tragic: the kids were shooting skyrockets along the streetcar tracks and one skyrocket veered off the track and went towards the Florida Grill. Victor Grieco and a friend, Wally Zenuk, were standing there and ducked when it came towards them. The skyrocket hit the window and then turned and struck Wally on the side of his head. Victor pulled the skyrocket out of his head, and with the help of their friends they got him into a car and rushed him to Western Hospital on Bathurst Street. News of the accident spread fast and we all rushed to the hospital.

Wally died that night. The police were there and were questioning everybody. Well, the newspaper played it up good, and the police were saying it was a gang fight between the Italians and the Jewish kids from Spadina Avenue. That was a lot of bunk; the kids were just having fun, and who could have predicted that something like this would happen? The Spadina kids were doing the same thing, but it was not a "war" between them. They were all having fun shooting rockets along the tracks, throwing firecrackers under the streetcars, and scaring the passengers. I'm not saying what they were doing was right, but the thought of anybody getting hurt hadn't occurred to them. It was after this incident that skyrockets were banned from home use.

* * *

The Italians and the Jewish boys got along great. They were all cut from the same fabric. Most were raised by European parents, toughened up and streetwise as a result of hard times, always defending themselves and each other against the verbal abuses from the dominant group of that era, constantly being called "kikes", "sheenies", "hebs", "wops", "greasy wops", "dagos", "spaghetti benders" and "grease-balls".

Ever since the turn of the century, with the influx of immigrants who settled in the Ward, mostly Jews and Italians, there was this sense of bonding, sticking together, helping each other out in those times of gross discrimination. And even later on, when they started to move away from the Ward – the Jews to the Kensington area, the Italians to the College Street area – the camaraderie still existed.

One incident took place back in 1933. The Jewish boys were being attacked in Christie Pits Park by the "Pit Gang" after a ball game. When the word got out, the Italians rallied around to help them. Trucks were sent to the Ward to pick up old Jewish buddies, and to College and Clinton – Little Italy – to pick up the "boxing buddies" (Sammy Luftspring, the Italian guys – like Frankie Genovese, the Bagnato Brothers, Stevie Rocco) and others, like Johnny Lombardi. They brought baseball bats, pipes, broomsticks and anything else they could get their hands on. During that week (so the story goes), after the riot there was still some unrest by the Pit Gang, so a bunch of dump trucks carrying the "Mansfield Gang" (the Italians) circled the entire area of Christie Pits, driving along Bloor, Christie, Barton and Crawford. They stayed there as long as they had to in order to make their presence known. It worked, because it ended the problem. I can't imagine what would have happened if that were today; with the availability of guns, it could have been a real tragedy. In those days a grudge or argument between two people was usually settled with their fists.

Then there were the "kibby joints", where the older guys hung out. There was Beefy's Place ("Beefy" Spizzeri) on Clinton Street next to the Monarch Hotel, as well as Jake's (Jake Cancelli) at Manning and Henderson. The guys hung out, joked around, played a little cards, and generally socialized. Once in a while somebody would get hungry at Beefy's Place, and his brother "Weasel" would run down to Frediani's store and buy a couple of buns and a few cents worth of cold cuts and bring them back to make sandwiches. If these places could talk, they could tell quite a story – the shenanigans that went on, the kibitzing, the story telling, and the tricks they played on one another. I used to love listening to the stories about some of the hijinks they pulled. And the stories about Beefy Spizzeri and his brother Weasel, who never agreed on anything in their whole lives. The dialogue between them would have put Abbott and Costello, and Dean Martin and Jerry Lewis, to shame.

Believe me, there was always a story to tell. One night George Pasquale put on a blonde wig and a dress and sat in the back seat of Augie Cusimano's car, with Augie at the wheel. They slowly drove all around the neighbourhood passing in front of the Florida Grill. The guys thought Augie had a girl in the car and started to follow him all around the streets to see who the new girl was; if there was a new broad around, they wanted in on the action. Of course Augie and George were killing themselves laughing. Another time, Big Mike DiBari had a barbecue in his back yard and invited a few friends over. Danny DiFlorio heard about it, and because he wasn't invited he called the fire station and said there was a fire raging out of control at 33 Clinton Street. The fire trucks raced to the house and saw that it was a joke. They didn't think it was very funny and demanded to know who had called. Of course, nobody knew.

* * *

Above, from left to right: My cousin George Vertolli and his wife, Leona White, Tony Marinangeli, and his sister and friends

Right: Horsing around on College Street, clockwise from the top: Wilfred Pasquale, Tony DeLuca and Jimmy Zuppo

Opposite page, left: from left to right: My brother Lou, Lillian Larsen, and my sister Pat

Opposite page, right: Some of the guys hanging out in front of Jake's kibby joint

Above left: Jake Cancelli (of Jake's kibby joint)

Above right: My friends Lillian Larsen (left) and Frances Crimo (later my maid of honour) in our back yard

Left: Angelo Gabriele and Maria Luigina Grimaldi, our local postmasters

Opposite page, top: Mr. Stoyanoff ("Lumbo") in front of his Florida Grill on College Street

Opposite page, bottom: Maria Luigina Grimaldi in front of her post office on Bellwoods Avenue

Emilio "Buffy Valentine" Valentini standing in front of his store on College Street. From shining shoes to co-owning the King Edward Hotel: "Who would believe it?"

Josephine Ball standing on the corner of Manning and College

Cappuccitti's grocery store on the corner of Claremont and Treford Place

Cheering for Buffy Valentine's baseball team, "Club U", at Trinity Bellwoods Park. Among the fans I recognize are Peter Grieco, Joe Prospero, Bertie Mignacco, Nick Lofranco, Buffy Valentine and Sam Demacio

The Club Bernard baseball team, one of many in the community

Members of Club Bernard receiving an award. Left to right: Luigi Spadacini, Mario Giorlando (my uncle), Mike Tanti, Vic Bernard, and (unknown)

Opposite page, top: Club Kallie. Top row, left to right: Peter Collini, Dave Antonacci, Vincent Trauzzi, Alfie Loreti, Johnny Dario, Mike Pesce, Freddie Maddalena. Bottom row, left to right: Mike Dibonis, Joseph Chiappetta, Jimmy Pesce, Johnny LoFeodo, Arthur Chiappetta

Opposite page, bottom: Club Kallie father and son banquet, second anniversary party

Scenes from the Columbus Boys Club. Left to right: the Club building on Bellwoods Avenue; floor hockey game; the pool table and trampoline in the Club's basement

Below: a Club newsletter

Opposite page: The kids always enjoyed the Club's Saturday night movies

Al "Robbie" Robertson was a talented boxer and also a popular entertainer, shown above performing as "Fifi the Clown" for the kids at the Boys Club

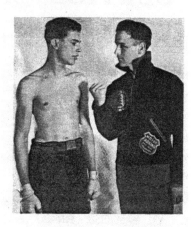

Ernie White   Robbie Robertson
in Training for
1944 Canadian Army Championships

Carmen Bush, a member of Canada's Baseball Hall of Fame, was the Club's sports director for many years

Below: In his earlier days, the Columbus Boys Club's founding director Hector MacNeil played hockey at the famed University of Notre Dame

Our neighbourhood children used to parade around our streets playing their makeshift musical instruments. This photo was taken in or around 1937.

Left to right: (Unknown), (Unknown), Joe Diacova, Freddie Maddalena, Ernie Vertolli, Patsy Loreti, Joe Vertolli, Ernie Loreti, Jimmy Zuppo, Louis Jannetta, Alfie Loreti

Johnny Lombardi & His Orchestra

Johnny Lombardi: musician, grocer, broadcaster and founder of Chin Radio – a true pillar of the community

Some say *he's top noodle*
in the macaroni business

The unofficial mayor of Little Italy

Lombardi, who emcees his Massey Hall shows, radiates warmth and geniality

By BRIAN MAGNER

At Dorsay's Shoe Shine, Dorsay used to play the guitar between customers. Left to right: George Pasquale, "Boots" Coseni, Dorsay, and Rudy Pasquale.

* * *

The stories go on. All the younger guys wanted to be like the older guys, although some of these younger guys had enough stories of their own to tell. And the teenagers wanted to be like the younger guys, and so on. One thing about our neighbourhood, there was always something going on. The DiMarco family, who lived on Clinton (some of the family still live there), had some property in Clarkson, Ontario. They would organize a corn roast and whoever was going would meet on Clinton Street and pile onto Carmen Leone's flatbed truck.

Then there were the ball games in Trinity Bellwoods Park. We used to go and watch Buffy Valentine's "Club U" play against other club's teams, and if Club U won, the players used to form a circle and sing "Little Liza Jane". After the game we would sometimes go to Shapiro's Delicatessen at College and Beatrice, where the Standard is today, for a corned beef sandwich, which cost only 55 cents for two.

We actually spent a lot of time in Trinity Bellwoods Park, winter and summer. As far back as I can remember, as younger children in the winter, we used old washing-machine lids or cardboard boxes to slide down the hills. There was one hill we called the "king's hill"; halfway down, there was this big huge bump and when you went over it you really flew into the air. We got bumped and bruised, but we were young and we didn't care. We also skied down the hill on our homemade skis that we made out of barrel rungs. In the summertime we used to play baseball amongst ourselves and in general we horsed around. In those days, we felt safe at all times. As we got older, we walked through the park with our boyfriends. Later on, when we got married and had children, we walked with our baby carriages in the park with friends.

All the guys hung around at the pool room at the Florida Grill, which was next door to where Bar Italia now stands on College. It was run by Mr. Stoyanoff, a very nice Macedonian man nicknamed "Lumbo", so it was often referred to as Lumbo's pool room. The family lived upstairs and they were like family to the guys. There were a lot of places for the guys to hang out. There was Dorsay's Shoe Shine and Buffy's Shoe Shine. "Buffy Valentine" was what everyone called him, but his real name was Emilio Valentini. He was always scraping and scrambling to make a buck. Who could imagine at the time that later on, he and a partner would be in a position to buy the King Edward Hotel? (Which they did and later sold.) Vic Bernard had a custom tailoring shop where the guys used to hang out also. Sometimes they would raid his fridge while they were hanging out in the back room. One time he thought he would teach them a lesson. He made sandwiches out of dog food and placed them in the fridge. After they ate the sandwiches, he told them. That cured them!

There were "good guys" and "bad guys" – guys who wouldn't steal a nickel from anybody and guys who would steal anything that wasn't nailed down. They all hung out together and it didn't matter which path you took; everybody knew what the other guy did, but nobody judged. There were thieves, bookmakers, loan sharks, and bootleggers. They all grew up together and did whatever they had to do to survive, but there was no violence involved in their actions.

We congregated at the Purity Tea Room on College just east of Manning. It was run by two Macedonian brothers named George and Steve. We had many a delicious sandwich there (hot beef, western, and grilled cheese) with French fries and milkshakes and sundaes. These were the favourites then. Going there was like being with family; you knew everybody. If you didn't have enough money to pay for your order, they would trust you to pay later. We also went to the Daisy Tea Room (now Sneaky Dee's) at Bathurst and College for their Boston cream pie. It was the best. Another favourite place on College Street was Mars "Out of This World" Restaurant, which is still there to this day. We also hung out at the new restaurant that had opened up across the street from the Purity Tea Room called the Swell Dell.

We played the jukebox a lot. We all had favourite songs. At that time I liked "You Belong To My Heart" by Mart Kenney and His

Western Gentlemen with Norma Locke, and "To Each His Own" by The Ink Spots. Butchie Bagnato liked "Nancy (with the Laughing Face)" by Frank Sinatra. Johnny Tanzola liked "I'm Always Chasing Rainbows" by Perry Como, and my cousin Sammy Vertolli liked "Don't Fence Me In" by Bing Crosby and the Andrews Sisters. We played these records over and over. It's amazing how we were able to hang around for hours playing records, just ordering a Coke.

One year we decided to have a New Year's Eve party, and it was to be at the DeLuca house on Gore Street. We were all about fifteen years old. Our parents all agreed to let us go because they knew Mr. and Mrs. DeLuca would be there. We all chipped in some money to buy snacks and soft drinks. We made the mistake of giving the money to Butchie Bagnato, who blew it on a horse, so we all had to chip in again.

We were excited about the party. Eleanor Palladini and I went to Rose's Dress Shop and bought black crepe dresses with pearl studs, which were very popular then. We had a lot of fun at the party. We played records and danced and played "Spin the Bottle" – and the kissing was done in the hall, with the door closed. When Mr. or Mrs. DeLuca had to go to the washroom upstairs, one of us would go to the door and say, "Ix-nay." So much for the chaperoning, but it was all innocent fun.

After the party we walked home, because we all lived close by. In those years we were never afraid of walking at night in our neighbourhood. I usually had to be home by a certain time, but sometimes I wanted to stay out later, especially if we were having fun with the gang. I knew I'd get whacked, but I didn't care. One time, I told my mother I had to go to the drug store to get some personal things. What I really wanted to do was meet my friends at the King Theatre at Manning and College. While we were watching the movie, one of my friends said, "Hey, Rose, your mother is here." I thought, "Uh-oh, I'm going to get it." When I turned around to look at her, she was standing there akimbo in the back of the theatre. She said, "La drug-a stora, eh?" and she turned around and walked out. She just wanted to let me know that I hadn't fooled her. One thing about my mother was that she would never embarrass me in front of my friends.

Going to a neighbourhood theatre in those years was a far cry from going to a theatre today. When you go to see a movie today, you walk into a theatre full of strangers. In our day, you walked in and you knew everybody, even Mr. Lester, the manager. We kibitzed, we horsed around, a little smooching. The ushers never said anything to us unless some kids got really noisy. Some of the guys in our "gang" never paid admission. There were these two ushers that were twin brothers and for some reason they allowed our group to go in for free. Later on when the King Theatre closed, the new Pylon Theatre opened (now The Royal) and we started to go there. We were a couple of years older then, but it was the same thing: we knew almost everybody (but no free admission here, and I think we behaved a little better).

* * *

After the show we usually went to the Purity Tea Room or the Swell Dell. One day while Frances Crimo and I were in the Swell Dell, some of the boys came in. That was what they did – come in and then leave, go across the street to the Purity Tea Room, then off to Lumbo's pool room and some general fooling around on College. This time, all the guys left except Victor Grieco. He just sat there all by himself. When Frances and I got up to leave, he came over and asked if he could walk us home. Frances immediately said, "Sure Vic," and so he walked with us. When we got to Clinton Street, Frances said, "Why don't you two go for a walk? I'm tired, I'm going home." Well, I was giving her dirty looks because I didn't much like Vic at that time. So we went for a walk and then he walked me home. The next day I phoned Frances and gave her hell. She said, "What's wrong with you? He's a nice guy." And I said, "So why don't *you* go with him?" and she answered, "I would, but it's you he likes."

Well, it seemed every time we were at the Swell Dell or the Purity Tea Room, he was there and always asked to walk me home. After a while he sort of grew on me. The little things he talked about, the compassion he showed when he talked about the death of his little sister at the age of three months, in 1939. Her name was Mary Elizabeth, named after the Queen, who had just visited Canada that year. I would talk about my baby sister, who'd also died shortly after she was born, in 1935. He used to say, "If I ever have a daughter, her name will be Mary." Sometimes when we were walking and we would meet friends who were out with their baby in the carriage, he would want to pick up the baby, and he endeared himself to me.

Although he was a compassionate person, there was another side of him that I didn't like: He was very jealous. I worked at Markham and College; to get to work, I had to walk up Manning and along College to Markham, and coming home it was the same route. He didn't want me to walk down Manning because there was always a bunch of guys hanging out in front of Jake's kibby joint. For that matter, he didn't want me to walk up Clinton Street either because guys were always hanging out at Beefy's kibby joint. I guess he didn't want them looking at me. These guys were a little older than us and we pretty well knew them all and they were not disrespectful. Sure there was the odd "wolf whistle" or some other comment like, "Hubba, Hubba". Big deal, nobody minded and we probably would have felt slighted if they didn't comment. We used to have big arguments about this, and I would say to him, "If you don't want me to walk by the kibby joints, how do you expect me to get home? If you think I'm going to walk down Markham to Dundas and then along Dundas to Claremont and up Claremont, you're nuts!"

He also didn't want me to wear lipstick. His jealousy was a constant thorn in our relationship. One day we were walking along College and I met a guy from work and greeted him with a big smile and the usual small talk. Well, that started a really big argument. I mean, I worked with this guy every day and he was a really nice person. His name was Harvey; he was the shipper and we got along great. What was I supposed to do, ignore him? That's not me and nobody will make me be something I'm not.

Another time, I'd just got home from work and Vic phoned me and said, "How did you get home?" and I replied, "I walked home. How do you think I got home?" Vic said, "I was standing in front of Dorsay's place and I didn't see you walk by." And then he said, "Who drove you home?" I said, "I took a helicopter!" and hung up. I was so upset at him and my mother said, in broken English, "Why are you putting up with this nonsense? Next time he comes over I'm going to give him a piece of my mind!" I told Vic, "You better not come around for a while because my mother is really mad at you" – so what does he do? To see me, he would climb up Frediani's roof (at Claremont and Mansfield) and hop across seven or eight rooftops to get to my back bedroom window in the attic. One time my brother Lou came running upstairs to my room and said, "I heard someone on the roof," so he looked out the window and my heart was pounding wondering where Vic was. Well he was perched on the peak. So now I had to worry about him hopping on the roofs, wondering if he might fall – or, worse, my mother finding out.

One day I thought, I can't take this nonsense anymore. I decided to write him a "Dear John" letter. I left it on the windowsill of my bedroom. That night I went to see a show at the Pylon with my girlfriend Frances. When I came home the letter was torn in little pieces and left on the floor. He didn't come around for a while and I found I was missing him. If I saw him on College Street he would smile and walk the other way. Then one day he phoned and wanted to speak to me, so I met him on College and we walked and walked and talked and talked, and so we started to see each other again.

During our long walks, I learned a lot about Vic. He never made it past the fifth grade. He was kicked out of Grace Street Public School for always starting skirmishes and disrupting the class. He was sent down to Charles G. Fraser Public School. At that time a lot of the kids wore "skull caps" that they made from old grey felt fedora hats, worn by the men in those days. Some hats had buttons or bottle caps or studs on them and were very popular among young kids. These hats resembled the hat that Jughead wore in the Archie comic strips. When

Vic's teacher saw the hat, he pulled it off his head. Vic retaliated and was kicked out of that school, too.

At that time his family moved from Henderson to Clinton and Barton, but Victor still went down Clinton to College to be with his friends, even though his father forbade him to do so. One day his father chained him to the backyard fence to keep him from going, because he thought Vic's friends were a bad influence on him. So Victor pulled the fencepost out of the ground and went down to College Street, chain and all. The police saw him and questioned him and Vic explained to them what his father had done. The policemen put him in the cruiser and brought him home. They told his father that if he ever did that to Victor again, they would put *him* in jail.

Victor then went to work on a farm in Clinton, Ontario, for $25 a week. His chores there included ploughing the fields and milking the cows, etc. He really enjoyed it. When he returned home, he got a job at Loblaw's on Fleet Street. Then he was called up by the army to register, but was rejected. He did not return to his job at Loblaw's, even though a representative came to his home to try to convince him. It was a decision he later regretted.

Hanging out with the guys again got him into trouble with the law – stealing cars to go "joy riding". He was caught, charged with car theft, and sent to a reformatory. It was around this time, after he was released from the reformatory, and back on College Street, that he first had eyes for me.

Victor got a job driving a stake truck for Gus Longo at the food terminal, delivering produce. He enjoyed that action and decided to buy his own truck. He went to Gorrie's Downtown Chevrolet Oldsmobile and saw a good used Rugby stake truck for $600. He asked his parents for a loan to buy the truck. His mother was all for it, but his father was not. In a way, you could understand his way of thinking. If they had a little money put away, they must have scrimped and sacrificed to save for a rainy day. And because Vic was a bit of a rebel, they were reluctant to have faith in him. He was hurt and upset. As winter approached and the market slowed up, he was let go.

He eased up a little on the jealousy issue and by now we were going pretty steady. Even Mamma noticed the difference.

* * *

I remember Mamma would say to me, "Sometimes you have to do things you don't want to, to set things straight." Like she had when I was giving her my whole pay and she asked me not to tell Pa. He thought I was only paying room and board. If he knew I was giving her all my pay, he would have given her a little less. Many times he would ask me to give a little more. What could I say? Pat was very angry at this and said, "It's not right. You're getting hell from Pa for nothing!" I can understand my mother having to do this. And now thinking about it, I could also understand why my father had to have a little money – not that he was a big spender. He didn't gamble, but he did like to go to the show sometimes. He liked the Tarzan movies. He also liked to go to the men's club in the basement of St. Agnes Church for a little friendly socializing with his *paesans*, and sometimes on the weekends he liked going to the Monarch Hotel for a beer with his friends. When you have worked on construction all week, you need a little diversion to help get you through. There has to be a balance in life to survive.

The women had their own way of coping, too – chitchatting over a cup of coffee with neighbours, maybe a little idle gossip, doing the "*malocchio*" (evil eye) prayers. I'll try to define the *malocchio* as simply as possible: The whole concept is that someone is knowingly wishing you misfortune, or, on the other hand, someone has unintentionally and without malice given you the *malocchio*. This is done by paying someone a compliment and not saying, "God bless you." Growing up, I always remember the Italian ladies saying, "How beautiful you are, God bless you." ("Come sei bella, benedica.")

At first my mother did not believe in the *malocchio* and thought it was nonsense. One time she had a very bad migraine that would not go away. Her friend insisted she had the *malocchio* and wanted to help her, but Mamma wanted no part of it. After a few more days of suffering with her headache, she gave in and had it done. To her surprise, the headache vanished and she became a firm believer. Now *she* wanted to be able to do this. She had to learn the prayers on Christmas Eve, as that was, and still is, the belief.

So every time we had a headache or were feeling sick, my mother would say, you might have the *malocchio*. There was a way to determine whether it was done intentionally or not. There were different ways to do the *malocchio* prayers; this was my mother's way: First of all, she would sit you down beside the table, which had a soup plate filled with water. Next she would start praying while making the sign of the cross on your forehead several times. Then came the olive oil, which she would drop from a spoon onto the plate of water, one drop at a time. With each drop she watched it carefully before dropping another. It was important to see how the drops formed in the water – a single drop intact, two drops joining together, or drops dispersing immediately when dropped into the water – that's what would help her determine whether or not it was done intentionally. After all this, she would say, "Now sit there and relax, and you will start yawning and then when this happens, the evil eye will be gone." Sure enough, whether it was the power of suggestion or not, we would start to yawn and my mother would say, "Now you'll feel better." It was common in those days for a neighbour, or someone who had a friend that was not feeling well, to come to our house and say to my mother, "Andoniella, can you do the malocchio?"

There was this older English woman who used to fix sewing machines. All the women in the neighbourhood used to call her when they couldn't fix their machines themselves. When they called, she would say, "Try to get three or four ladies together and I will read your tea leaves for twenty-five cents each." Getting your sewing machine fixed and having your tea leaves read was a little social gathering for them.

As I mentioned before, they had their own way of coping

with the stresses of life. Simple things, but it got them through. The difference between then and now is that they didn't expect any more out of life. One day while she was there, my mother wanted her to read my cup, too. I said, "Ma, save your quarter, I don't believe in this." But she insisted and the lady said, "I would really like to read your tea cup." So I gave in reluctantly. After much concentration, the lady said, "You will have a very fulfilling life, but a bumpy road along the way, but you will become rich and famous." I turned to my mother, who had a big smile on her face and said, "See Ma, I told you, you should have saved your quarter!"

Being young and living through lean years, the "rich and famous" part was a fantasy, but the bumpy road and overcoming the hurdles was true enough, and I must say that my life has been fulfilling. I guess two out of four wasn't bad. Although if you define rich as in having a great family and great friends, and not in a monetary sense, then yes, I would say I am rich.

* * *

One day, in about 1946, Vic and I were doing our usual thing, walking along College Street. We would stop and talk and then walk again and usually bump into friends that were also out walking. This is what we did. We were standing in front of the Nemo building at College and Manning and the police came up to us and told us to move on. Move on! Can you imagine that? Here we are walking in our own neighbourhood where we were born and raised, and they tell us to move on! I guess the stigma during World War Two of being Italian was still with us. They may as well have come into our homes and told us to move on, because College Street was like our second home.

It wasn't just us kids that the police bothered. Any group of men, especially Italian men, just hanging out and talking, were also told to move on. Meeting friends, and hanging out and socializing is what our neighbourhood was all about. You must remember in those years, not too many had cars; there were no TVs, computers, video games, etc.

Our entertainment was meeting friends. College Street was our *piazza* (town square), for young and old alike. They came from Claremont, Bellwoods, Treford, Manning, Grace, Euclid, Montrose, Mansfield, Crawford, Roxton – and you knew everybody.

If the police thought that strolling through our own neighbourhood was a threat, I wonder what they would think of the Toronto of today. I'm not saying we didn't have crimes in our day, but they were few and far between. Lord knows, we had some dandies.

In 1949, Edwin Alonzo Boyd robbed his first bank, the Bank of Montreal at College and Manning. He went on to rob several more banks successfully without firing a gun. In October 1951 he robbed the Dominion Bank at Lawrence and Yonge and was caught. In the Don Jail, he soon hooked up with Lennie Jackson and Willie Jackson (not related). On November 5th, Edwin Boyd, Lennie Jackson and Willie Jackson escaped. "The Boyd Gang" (as they were named at that time by Jocko Thomas, Toronto Daily Star crime reporter) went on to rob several banks. As fate would have it, on March 6th, 1952, Detective Edmund Tong and Sergeant Roy Perry stopped a car near College and Lansdowne, and in the car were Lennie Jackson and another man, Steve Suchan. I guess the policemen didn't expect any trouble, because their guns were not drawn, but as they approached the car, they were greeted with a hail of bullets. Detective Tong died two weeks later. Tips from the underworld led police to Montreal, where they arrested both Jackson and Suchan. Shortly after that, the police found out the whereabouts of Boyd and arrested him also.

They were all sent back to the Don Jail, but not for long. If you can believe it, on September 7th, 1952, the Boyd Gang escaped for the second time. Now, working around the clock and getting tips from the public, they zeroed in on a barn in North York and arrested them without incident. Boyd was sentenced to life in prison. Steve Suchan and Lennie Jackson were hung in the gallows of the Don Jail on December 16th, 1952, for the murder of Detective Edmund Tong. Edwin Alonzo Boyd died in 2002 at age 88 and a movie has been made about him.

We had our share of boosters, thieves, bootleggers, bookmakers, loan sharks and wannabe "wise guys". If there was a certain item that you wanted, the boosters were around to take your order. If you needed money in a hurry, there were the loan sharks. Roy, the "loan arranger", was a no-nonsense guy. If you owed him money, you had better pay him back. Sometimes he used to rub people the wrong way. One time the word was out that there was going to be a fight between Roy and Carmen Leone. All the guys in the neighbourhood were anxiously awaiting the big event. They were taking bets on who would win. Carmen, who took boxing lessons at the Columbus Boys Club, won the fight hands down, and Roy ended up with a broken nose. The next morning, Carmen went to Roy's house and apologized for breaking his nose. Another time, there was going to be a fight between Roy and Frankie Genovese, but the fight was called off. They say Frankie would have won the fight with one hand tied behind his back.

Roy had his finger in a lot of things; some say he had ties with the mob. At one time he owned a paving company and did a job for someone who then refused to pay him. No problem. He just got a pick and broke up all the new pavement – simple as that. But that was Roy. He had a certain charm, and he was very charismatic; the women loved him. But with all his wheeling and dealing, the booze got the better of him; he wound up shooting his estranged wife, and then himself.

* * *

Never a dull moment in our neighbourhood. You would walk down the street and see the Italian men playing *morra* outside and smoking their Marco Gallo cigars. Or the younger kids playing "Buck Buck, How Many Fingers Up?" You could walk down the back lanes and always find a crap game going on. As kids, we walked up and down the lanes to find our treasures. There were no garage sales or lawn sales. We used to go into the Jewish area because they had the best treasures. We called them the "lucky lanes".

We had a lot of good talent. Buck Bernard had a powerful

operatic voice. When he sang, the whole neighbourhood could hear him. Frank Pasquale also had a good operatic voice, as well as his brother Wilfred, who was more of a crooner. Natalie Tamburano had a lovely voice; she won on talent night at the King Theatre. My sister Eleanor also had a great voice and Mamma sent her for singing lessons. Another talent was Frank Locicero, nicknamed "Frankie Laine", because he sounded just like him. Another great singer was Paul Rosa who sang at various functions; later, at the age of 90, he appeared in the Chartwell Senior Star Talent Show.

We also had our fair share of good boxers. Thanks to the Columbus Boys Club for that! The Bagnato brothers were also very involved in training, promoting, etc. They trained out of the Diamond Boxing Club, at Dufferin and St. Clair, owned by Peter Calderone, and the Lansdowne Athletic Club on Wade Avenue, owned by Bertie Mignacco; there was also Sully's on Ossington Avenue.

They fought amateur bouts at Massey Hall and later some of them went on to Patterson, New Jersey, to train and fight there. To name a few, there was Joey (Stushy) Bagnato, who became a Canadian lightweight contender. Rudy (Pascoe) Pasquale was also probably just a couple of fights away from being a champ; he attracted the attention of the big promoters from New York City and fought at Madison Square Garden. He eventually had to quit boxing because of brittle hands. His brother, Wilfred (Xavier) Pasquale had a promising career in boxing, too. He was a classic boxer, not a slugger. En route to a boxing bout in Peterborough, Ontario, they were in a car accident. Although there were no serious injuries, Wilfred wound up with a concussion. The boxing bouts were cancelled and Wilfred never returned to boxing after that accident. It was a good thing, because it would have been awful to see that handsome face beat up.

There were other really good boxers, like Frankie Pucci, Val Mancuso, Frankie Genovese, Frankie Brancetti, Frank (Cordino) Cortese. Then there was Sammy Luftspring from Spadina Avenue, and further west in the Junction was George Chuvalo, who went on to become the Canadian amateur heavyweight champion in 1955, and as a professional he won the Canadian heavyweight title in 1958! These guys should have been in Hollywood; they sure were a handsome bunch. When Frankie Genovese won a fight and had a few bucks on him, he would go into Jake's kibby joint. He'd call all the kids on the street to come in and he would treat them to an ice cream cone. The double-headers were five cents.

We sure had some lovable characters. Many times at Christmas, Mr. Pasquale dressed in a Santa Claus suit and rode up and down our streets with a horse and sleigh. There was Mrs. Magnacca, who looked like "Granny" from the comic strip of that name. She would walk up and down the street knitting socks, and when she got tired of knitting she would stick the knitting needles in the bun at the back of her head. There was Rocky Pasquino (we called him "Oink") – he was something else. He served some time in the army; one day he was so hungry he raided the sergeant's mess and ate thirty-five sausages and a dozen eggs. Then he said, "I can't help it, I love to eat!" Rocky was honourably discharged from the army. He didn't live in our neighbourhood but was well known. He was very mannerly and never bothered anyone. Sometimes he was able to get a handout from the stores or from people in our neighbourhood. Many times my mother would make tomato sandwiches from our garden for him and he would forever thank her. Often he would put on a show for us. He would pick up anything and balance it on his head. He once picked up a ladder and balanced it on his head and the people gave him food. He entered the hotdog-eating contest at the C.N.E. and won hands down. He even made it into the newspaper.

One night Rocky was feeling a little hungry but had no money. He went to see his buddy George "Butchie" Bagnato, who never refused to help someone with a handout, or lend money to a friend. Butchie took him to the Purity Tea Room and told him to order anything he wanted. Big mistake! Rocky ate his way through two hot chicken sandwiches, two hot beef sandwiches, three hot hamburger sandwiches, (bear in mind these sandwiches were served with mashed potatoes, peas, and gravy), ten donuts, two pieces of cake, five cups of coffee and three large Cokes. Butchie picked up a whopping bill of $3.45. You can bet your life he had a snack before he went to bed. And how could we talk about our neighbourhood without mentioning Dorothy O'Brien, the eyes and ears of the neighbourhood? She knew everything that went on; you couldn't walk by her house (if she was standing there, which she usually was!) without getting an earful about someone or something. I have to say she certainly added flavour to the neighbourhood!

In our area, almost everybody had a nickname. You could know somebody your whole life by their nickname and never know their real names. I'll give you a rundown of some of the names I can remember:

"Beefy" Spizzeri

"Weasel" Spizzeri

"Beaky" Pesce

"Popeye" Pillo

"Blackie" Coseni

"Boots" Coseni

"Spinach" Domenici

"Willie the Hop" Roncetti

"Nicole the Wop" Roberto

"Pete the Brain" D'Agostino

"Pete the Bug" Panzini

"Louie the Liar" Gerardi

"The Frog" Bartucco

"Smiley" Cancelli

"Dick O'Toole" Cancelli

Ernie "Sleepy" Vertolli

Luciano "Slim" Vertolli

"Mandrake the Magician" Iannacci

"Flatty" DiFlorio

"Bumps" DiFlorio

"Papa" Ryan

"Dapper Lou" Benedetti

"Paniotta" Antonacci

"Mousey" Maiola

"Vic the Bullshitter" D'Andrea

"Chink" Micelli

"Chellagher" Micelli

Lou"The Weeper" Muccili

John "Dusty" DiLeo

"Banjo" DiLeo

"Rooster" DiLeo

"Butch" Ziccari

"Teetles" Ziccari

"Butchie" Bagnato

"G Man" Diacova

"Louie the Tout" Giuffre

"Butler" DelDuca

"Angel" Veltri

"Chopper"

"Chicken" or "Gallina"

"Dago Kelly"

"Snow White" Tanzola

"Needle Nose" Domenici

"The Silver Fox" Grieco

"Doc" Gentile

"Boom Boom" Decina

"Chippy" Chiappetta

Tony "Eggie" Lofranco

"Corky" Cortese

"Joe the Dipper"

"Downtown George"

"Ansalada" Locicero

"The Whisperer" Bigelli

And last but not least, my husband… Victor "The Gypsy" Grieco. He was given that name by Larry Patrick when he was fifteen years old (because he looked like the good-looking gypsies that used to hang out on Queen Street) and it stayed with him for life.

* * *

Opposite page: In front of Marinangeli's grocery store, some of the guys in their younger years. Left to right: Rudy Leone, Victor Grieco, Tony Marinangeli, Sammy Brancetti

Victor "The Gypsy" Grieco. "What a hunk!"

Top: Me at age sixteen.

Above left: Clara and Mary Quaranto and me in front of Queen's Park

Above right: My cousin Mary Vertolli, Laura Trauzzi, Rose Crimo, and my sister Pat Vertolli at the Belt Manufacturing Company, where they worked

Me again, in 1948 at Trinity Bellwoods Park

Top left: Norma and Lillian Larsen and friends

Top right: Me at the Crawford Street bridge

Opposite page: Victor and me at the Humber River, one of our favourite swimming spots

Following page: Victor being very romantic on the beach at the Humber River. "Those were the days, my friends..."

* * *

In 1947, one night after a show, when Victor took me home my mother was waiting for us in the hallway. She looked at us and said, "Mah, you two gonna marry, or what?" She took us completely by surprise. Vic looked at me and said, "You know, she's right!" And *that was my proposal!* Now wasn't that romantic? So much for, "Darling, will you marry me?"

Come to think of it, the two most important decisions in my life (which should have been mine to make) were made by my mother: Whether or not to go to high school and further my education, and then not waiting to have a memorable and romantic proposal. I guess it was the right decision because our marriage lasted for sixty-one years, until Vic's passing.

We called our friend Joe Nodell to make my engagement ring; this was the former Joe Nobleman from the Belt Manufacturing Company; he changed his name when he started his business. Victor had some diamonds that he said he won in a crap game and he gave them to Joe. When Joe brought Vic the ring, we went to the Purity Tea Room and ordered a Coke and Vic put the ring on my finger. The next day, I couldn't wait to go to work and announce my engagement and show my ring to everybody. I remember how impressed they were.

We decided to get married in December. I wanted to get married at St. Agnes Church, where my parents were married. Vic, who was Pentecostal, was willing to do whateveR the priest asked of him so that we could be married there. But the priest said he would not allow it because December is the month of Advent. Then he asked me if I was pregnant, as they did allow December weddings under "special circumstances", but I said no. I could have said yes, but I didn't want to start my marriage with a lie. So we made arrangements at the Church of All Nations, at Queen and Spadina, to be wed on December 13th.

I took one week off work. My co-workers at the factory gave me a party. They set up at the cutting table and ordered rye bread, pastrami, corned beef and pickles, and rye whiskey and pop. They all pitched in and gave me some money. All the workers in the next department came over to congratulate me.

Preparing for our wedding was not a big deal. Vic brought me a bale of houndstooth fabric. He said he "acquired" it somewhere. I took it to Vic Bernard's Custom Tailoring Shop on College Street and had my "going away" suit made. I bought my white satin wedding gown at the Town and Country Shop on Yonge Street for $35. My maid of honour, Frances Crimo, bought a blue satin gown in the same style. I had to lend her three dollars to put down on it.

Victor and our best man, Wilfred Pasquale, rented tuxedos. When it came time to go to the church, the boys left first. We hadn't arranged for a car of my own, so Uncle Mario went up the street to Jake's kibby joint and got "Dick O'Toole" Cancelli to drive Frances and me to the church. We waited at the church for a while, wondering where Victor and Wilfred were. It turns out they were at Lumbo's pool room showing off their tuxedos.

We had the wedding reception at my house. We'd ordered cold cuts and buns from the DeFilippo's store across the street from us. We invited some neighbours, friends, relatives, *comares* and *compares* and my friends. Sammy Antonacci, who lived three doors away from us, came over with his accordion and played. I didn't ask him, I didn't hire him; he just came over and played. Pure and simple, and that's what our neighbourhood was all about. It was wonderful. We didn't have much money so we couldn't plan ahead, but we did reserve a room at the King Edward Hotel for that night.

We really wanted to go to Niagara Falls for a couple of days and stay at the General Brock Hotel, which was the norm at that time, but we had to wait to see if we would receive any money as gifts. As it turned out, Vic's brother Joe gave us a cheque for $50. We were ecstatic; that was almost two weeks wages at that time. We also received a little more money, so now we could plan our honeymoon.

We left $65 with my sister Pat, so that we would have some money when we got home. When we arrived in Niagara Falls, we visited our old family friends Joe and Rose D'Amore, who could not attend the wedding but asked us to visit. We also visited their son Hank and daughter Carm and her husband Dave Dawson.

We needed to make reservations at the General Brock Hotel. When we called, we found out the cost of a room was eleven dollars a night. My friend Rose said, "That's too much. My friend owns a tourist home, let me check to see if there are any vacancies." Luckily enough there were, and we were able to get a beautiful room and bath for $3.50 a night. We were really happy. Now we could afford to go to the Town Casino in Buffalo, and for $1.50 we saw a wonderful show and had a great dinner. Back in Niagara Falls, our friends Carm and Dave took us to the Venetian Hotel, where Dave worked, and we had really good hot chili and ice-cold draught beer, and had a really great time. We stayed in Niagara Falls for five days.

When we got back to Toronto, we moved into my bedroom in the attic, which I fixed up before we left to look really pretty. I got some orange crates from the grocery store and made a vanity with some lovely chintz material. I put new sheets on my bed before I went on my honeymoon, so that my room would be nice when we came back. We lived in that attic for two years, and when the middle room on the second floor became available we moved in there. Then when my brother and his wife moved out, we were able to take the back room on the second floor as well, so we made it into a kitchen. Boy, was I happy to have two rooms! We bought a stove and a chrome table with six chairs. It was great having our own space and inviting my friends over. Before that, when my friends visited we'd stay downstairs with my family, but this was more private.

* * *

In the 50s, another surge of immigrants arrived in Toronto. By then the economy was getting better and they really did come to a land of opportunity. In time, a lot of different nationalities settled in Toronto's Little Italy, and there were never any racial problems. I can't think of anybody who did more than Johnny Lombardi to have united multiculturalism and multilingualism with his CHIN radio station. He knew what discrimination was all about. He lived it – experienced it – and he took a chance. Johnny Lombardi was part of our neighbourhood for as far back as I can remember. His love of music helped him get through those tough years, as it did for most of us Italians. Life without music was no life at all. When Johnny had to have an operation, a few of the young guys, including my brother, donated their blood for him, as they did for anybody else in our neighbourhood who needed it.

Johnny went on to open his first grocery store in 1946 at Manning and Dundas, then at College and Clinton. As business improved he opened a huge supermarket on College near Grace. In 1966, he started his radio station in a little office above the supermarket. In time he needed more space and acquired a larger building across the street at 622 College – and the rest is history.

Just below College on Grace, there is a statue of Johnny sitting on a bench with his legs crossed, looking very relaxed. Also sitting on the bench is a statue of a little boy – a little boy who had a dream. Above the statue are three guardian angels that appear to be watching over them; every Christmas they have the lighting of the angels, and all the people in the neighbourhood join in to celebrate this.

Little Italy's College Street, between Clinton and Grace, is appropriately named Johnny Lombardi Way.

* * *

We socialized a lot with friends – young married couples just starting out on their own, sometimes living at home for a while or renting a flat. Visiting friends who lived in flats was normal in those days.

My friends Caroline and Lena Tanti both lived in their mother-in-law's flat on Gore Street. Lena had a seven-year-old daughter who had to share her parent's bedroom. They all shared a tiny kitchen. When I think back on those years, I wonder how six or eight people could fit around the table, which took up most of the kitchen. We kibitzed around, we played cards, and around eleven o'clock somebody would get hungry and out came the spaghetti pot, because there was always some tomato sauce in the fridge. Trying to cook in that tiny kitchen with all of us there, was poetry in motion. Those were the days!

A group of the girls decided to have a weekly card game. They asked me to join and taught me how to play poker. We played every Thursday night and we each took our turn hosting. We'd start around seven p.m. and at midnight we'd serve food, and then continue on till two or three a.m. It didn't matter how late we played because we lived within minutes of each other. Clara Crooks lived next door from me, and my sister-in-law Irene lived upstairs in their flat. Lena Benedetti lived next to Clara, and Mary Bernard lived upstairs in Lena's flat; Mary moved later to Treford Place (just around the corner). The furthest one was Vi Tibando, Lena's sister in-law, who lived on College near Brunswick, upstairs from her mother-in-law's grocery store, called Tibando's. We played Pogey Poker, which means you could not lose more than one dollar and you got to stay in the game. I looked so forward to those weekly card games, even though I had to sit through a haze of smoke so thick you could cut the air with a knife.

In those years smoking was not an issue; nobody said it was harmful to our health. I remember my brothers and sister making roll-your-own cigarettes with a "V-Master" gadget. They bought tobacco and cigarette papers and rolled long cigarettes and cut them to size. There were some cigarettes that were sold five in a pack, called Turrett. I never smoked. Sometimes when we were sitting on the veranda, Pat would hand me a cigarette and tell me to go in the house and light it on the gas stove, and she would say, "Inhale till it lights up." I used to hack and cough doing this, but you didn't say no to Pat.

It wasn't so much the card-playing that I enjoyed but the chitchat that went along with it – the humour and the conversation about any happenings in our neighbourhood. And believe me, there was one such incident that shocked the neighbourhood that still comes up even to this day. When our friends Dorothy and Sam decided to get married, they set their wedding date. There were months of preparation for the wedding – dress fittings, attending bridal showers – and everybody was looking forward to this happy event. On the night of Sam's stag, which was the day before the wedding, Dorothy's former boyfriend John Tanti called and asked her to meet him because he wanted to talk to her. She agreed to meet him and once she was in the car he drove nonstop to Montreal, and if you could believe it, they got married.

When word got back to Toronto, it was like a bomb was dropped on our neighbourhood. Nobody could believe it. Dorothy and John went on to have five children. Sam eventually got married and had a daughter. Later on, while at his summer cottage, Sam had been flying a kite along the beach shore, playing with the children; sadly, the kite wire touched a hydro wire and Sam was electrocuted and died instantly. Another bombshell; our whole neighbourhood was overwhelmed with grief.

Around this time, I became pregnant with my first child. In February of 1951, while playing poker at Mary Bernard's house on Treford Place, I was experiencing labour pains, but I still continued to play. When Mary served food at midnight I said to the girls, "Maybe I shouldn't eat any food, I might have to go to the hospital." Vi said, "Go ahead and eat. If you go to the hospital they will give you an enema anyway."

I continued to play until around two a.m. Walking home, the contractions were getting worse and I was hanging on to Lena. At that time Victor was driving cab (using his own car). When I got home I called the cab company and they called Vic on the two-way radio. On the way to the hospital, I didn't think I was going to make it and when I got there they took me right in to give birth; there was no time to prep me. I gave birth to a baby girl, who we named Mary Anne.

At that time there was a very bad influenza epidemic and we had to stay in the hospital for ten days, with no visitors. Half of the staff was away with the flu and only doctors were allowed in. When Victor brought me some personal things or some fruit, he had to leave them at the main floor desk. During our ten-day stay, two of my friends from the neighbourhood, Eleanor and Eva, who'd also just given birth, were brought into our room. It was great to see familiar faces.

When we were finally discharged, I was anxious to go home and have some homemade chicken soup, which I was sure Mamma would have ready, because that's what we did – good old homemade chicken soup, a cure-all for whatever ails you. To my great disappointment, Mamma was in bed with the flu and there was no chicken soup. Thank goodness for Pat, who was there for all of us. She lived close by on Henderson Avenue. She came over every day with her little daughter Janice to help me with the baby. One day while washing a glass, it broke and I got a nasty cut and had to have stitches. Because I couldn't get my hand wet, and because Mamma was still weak from the flu, Pat came every day to wash the diapers.

Victor worked the cab all night until six a.m. and then our friend Wilfred drove the cab all day. When Victor came home in the morning it was feeding time for the baby. Unfortunately, I was not able to nurse our child, so I had to feed her formula. Each night, I would prepare all the bottles for the next day and when Victor came home in the morning he would heat one and feed the baby. Every new mother would appreciate what it means to be able to sleep through the morning feeding. Vic was happy to do it.

It was at this time that Wilfred brought his new girlfriend Vicky Eftoff to meet us. She was a lovely Macedonian girl and I liked her immediately. I said to Wilfred, "She's a keeper, don't let this one go." When they got engaged and planned their wedding, they asked Victor to be the best man and me to be the "numka", a traditional Macedonian role, a notch above maid of honour. And we've remained close friends forever.

* * *

Vic soon had to quit cabbing because his car needed a lot of fixing. Small wonder, because the car was working day and night. He had a few jobs here and there. Sometimes he used to stay out late at night, but I never thought anything of it. In our neighbourhood, it was not that unusual. He always had money on him, and said he was lucky at shooting craps. That was also credible, because there was always a crap game going on at somebody's house or in the back lanes.

One night we were awoken at five a.m. when a couple of detectives knocked at our door and asked to speak to Vic. I asked Vic what was going on and he said, "Don't worry, honey, it's nothing." He started to whistle while he was getting dressed, and I learned at that moment that when he whistled a certain way I *should* be worried. He wasn't whistling a happy tune; it was more of a nervous reaction. With the events that followed I had every right to be worried. Victor and his buddies were charged with stealing a van loaded with fur coats.

Because Victor already had a police record, a friend suggested that I would need a good lawyer, and recommended the prominent Arthur Martin. My first meeting with Mr. Martin was friendly and very comfortable. He introduced us to his sister, who worked in the office, and to Mr. Pat Hart, a young gentleman who also worked with him.

In the days that followed, watching Mr. Martin in the courtroom – the respect he commanded upon entering, and everybody listening intently to every soft-spoken word – I was in awe of his performance.

Victor was allowed to leave on bail until his next court date. While out on bail, he and his buddy again got into trouble with the law, and were sent back to jail. Surprisingly, Mr. Martin did not condemn Victor for his poor choices. By then, I think he had taken a liking to us.

I said to Mr. Martin that I couldn't imagine where I was going to come up with more money to pay for further court costs and time. He said to me, "Did I ask you for more money? Don't worry about it." He continued to defend him at no further cost. He was a true gentleman.

Victor was incarcerated for approximately one year. While he was away, he wrote me many, many letters, many of them expressing his great regret for the mistakes he'd made. In one letter (dated June 16th, 1953), he wrote, "I feel a lot better since you visited me and hope you'll give me a chance to prove what I told you, because I love you very much." Later on in life, growing up and becoming a responsible citizen, Victor realized that having a police record was not a smart move. With owning your own business and applying for various licenses, there are always forms to fill out, and filling out a form that inquired--- about a police record was embarrassing. When you are young, you can't see past your nose and you suffer the consequences. But as the old saying goes, you live and you learn, which was why Victor was always trying to counsel the children and the grandchildren about the ramifications of doing foolish things and getting into trouble with the law.

You have to wonder why Victor turned out to be such a rebel, while his brother Joe remained very active in the church. Whatever it was that made Victor tick, despite his early rebellious days, his faults and misgivings, he was a kind, compassionate and giving person with a big heart.

* * *

In 1954 we had to move from Claremont Street. It was a very traumatic time for all of us. Victor and I didn't have the financial smarts to purchase the house, which was $11,000. Pa was not in the best of health at that time; he was experiencing mini epileptic seizures and couldn't work anymore. My parents took my three younger sisters and moved into my uncle's house on Manning Avenue. Vic and the baby and I moved into a three-bedroom apartment and took Sleepy, Joe and Eleanor with us. Leaving Claremont Street was like leaving a part of me behind. It took me a long time to get over it. Every time I walked by our house, my heart would turn over.

In 1956, we moved to my mother-in-law's flat on Barton Avenue. Victor and his buddy Al Malatesta started up their own paving business. In 1957, my second daughter Patricia Anne was born. We decided that we needed more space and in 1958 we bought the house that I still live in today. Victor and Al had a paving job on that street and they'd noticed the For Sale sign.

We moved in on December 1st. At midnight on New Year's Eve, we went out onto the veranda so we could beat our pots and pans together to ring in the New Year. This was our custom down on Claremont Street, but to our surprise there was no one out there, and it was very quiet. It was then that we realized this wasn't our old neighbourhood.

* * *

It seems there is a magnet that draws me back to the old district. What was it about our neighbourhood? Lord knows we certainly weren't born with a silver spoon, but there was something there.

Although most of us moved away, the camaraderie still exists. We still want to hang on to our youth; we don't want it to end, because there is a bond that can never be broken. A lot of our friends have passed away, but those who are left still get together and meet, some 60 to 70 years later. We never get tired of reminiscing about our buddies who've passed on, and about all the fun and kibitzing, the stories being told over and over again.

Every spring and fall, I get together with a group of girls from St. Francis School for lunch. And I'm in constant contact with my life-long friends, Teresa and Vicky. We've stuck by each other through thick and thin, all through the years. As I look back on my life, I feel I was very fortunate to have been a part of a large family. Sure, we had our ups and downs, but we also had our share of fun and love. We remember the bad times and laugh about them now, but mostly we remember the good times.

Growing up with them, and growing up in Little Italy, made me strong and prepared me for the life I was to lead, as a wife, mother, grandmother, business owner… But that's another story.

I certainly have no regrets, but sometimes I wish I would wake up to find that my life had only been a dream, and I am back to being that kid again. I would savour every moment of it.

Some of the gang...

Left to right: Rose Valentini, my sister Pat and me

My father and mother in our backyard garden on Claremont Street

Left to right: Our neighbour Evelyn Gentile, Mamma and Lillian Larsen

Paesans Angela Maria Vertolli and Mrs. DiTomasso with Mamma

Mamma with me and my five sisters. Clockwise from top left: Me, Eleanor, Pat, Gloria, Mary, Mamma and Joanie

Vic and me at a party, 1954

My parents, Riccardo and Josephine Vertolli, October 11, 1970, on their 50ᵗʰ wedding anniversary, with all ten of us, left to right: Mary, Gloria, Slim, Joanie, Lou, Pat, Sleepy, Joe, me, and Eleanor

Treasures from
My Mother's Kitchen

Insalata (Mixed Green Salad)

Babbaluci (Snails Cooked in Tomato Sauce)

Braciole (Beef Rolls in Tomato Sauce)

Carciofi Ripieni (Stuffed Artichokes)

Brodo di Pollo (Chicken Soup)

Cuccia (Wheat Berries with Honey)

Fresh Fava Bean Sauce

St. Joseph's Day Pasta

Groundhog Spezzatino

Meatballs

Pasta e Fagioli

Polenta

Spareribs with Savoy Cabbage

Sugo

Cucidati (Fig Cookies)

Insalata (Mixed Green Salad)

Enough greens to fill a large bowl (arugula, escarole, curly endive, leaf lettuce, radicchio), washed and drained

2 whole tomatoes and cucumbers, chopped (from the garden in the summer)

¼ cup olive oil

1 tbsp. red wine vinegar

½ tsp. salt

Pinch of pepper

Pinch of sugar

A small handful of fresh mint, chopped

Place all ingredients in a large bowl and gently toss. Season with salt and pepper to taste. On special occasions, Mamma would peel an orange and slice it very thin. Serves 12.

Babbaluci (Snails Cooked in Tomato Sauce)

100 snails (or 1 bushel)

1 cup cornmeal

10 fresh tomatoes, chopped

2 whole onions, diced

8 cloves garlic, crushed

4 tbsp. olive oil

½ bunch parsley, coarsely chopped

1 tsp. salt

1 loaf Italian bread

Soak snails in a bucket of cold water for 24 hours with a handful of cornmeal. Cover bucket with a heavy lid so snails don't escape! Put snails in a colander to drain water.

Heat a large pot with a tight fitting lid over medium heat. Heat olive oil over medium heat. Add onions and cook for two minutes, then add garlic and cook for one more minute. Add the tomatoes and salt and cook for five to ten minutes. Add the snails, cover with lid and steam for approximately five minutes. Finish with chopped parsley.

Serve in a large bowl with toothpicks to pluck the meat out of the shells. Serve with sliced Italian bread for dipping! Serves 12.

Braciole (Beef Rolls in Tomato Sauce)

2 lbs. beef leg (outside round), sliced thinly and pounded

½ lb. lard a pezzi (fatty piece of bacon)

3 cloves garlic, crushed

½ bunch, fresh parsley, chopped

1 tsp. salt

½ tsp. freshly ground pepper

¼ cup olive oil

Slice beef into 4-ounce pieces. Flatten slices with a mallet or the sides of a cleaver. Chop lard a pezzi until it forms a paste. Add in garlic, parsley, salt and pepper and continue to chop into a paste.

Lay beef slices out on a cutting board. Spread a thin layer of paste over the meat. Roll up and tie with butcher's twine so the meat doesn't unroll when cooking. Repeat until all pieces are assembled.

In a shallow frying pan over high heat, add olive oil and brown meat pieces on all sides.

Now the braciole are ready to be simmered for one hour in a pot of sugo, or until the meat is tender. Remove string before serving.

Sometimes my mother would use the uncooked meatball meat mixture instead of the larda pezzi, which is equally delicious. Serves 12.

Carciofi Ripieni (Stuffed Artichokes)

12 medium-size fresh artichokes

½ lemon, sliced

4 cups breadcrumbs

½ bunch fresh parsley, finely chopped

2 cloves garlic, finely chopped

⅓ cup Romano cheese, grated

1 tsp. salt

½ cup olive oil

¼ tsp. black pepper

Remove outer leaves of artichokes. Clip remaining points with scissors. Spoon out and remove inner choke. Trim stems so they will sit stem side down in the pan. Lightly compress and place in water with lemon until ready to stuff. Preheat oven to 350 degrees.

For the stuffing, place breadcrumbs, garlic, parsley, cheese, salt, pepper, and some of the olive oil into a bowl and mix until it's fully incorporated. Add a little water to mixture if it seems dry.

Stuff each artichoke until full. Make sure the stuffing gets in between all the leaves.

Place in pan, stem side down, so that the artichokes are close together and don't fall over. You can cut some potato wedges to keep everything upright if necessary. The tighter they fit in the pan, the better.

Add 1-inch depth of water to pan. Lightly top artichokes with a little olive oil and water to moisten. Cover and bake for 40 minutes until artichokes are cooked through. Test by pulling out an inner leaf. If it comes out easily, they are ready to eat. Serves 12.

Brodo di Pollo (Chicken Soup)

1 whole chicken, live or store-bought

2 whole onions, peeled and quartered

3 whole carrots, peeled and cut into large chunks

3 celery stalks, cut into large chunks

3 cloves garlic, peeled and crushed

3 oz. Romano cheese, piece of rind

Salt and pepper to taste

2 whole tomatoes, peeled and diced

1 large bay leaf

2 cups pastina or other pasta, cooked

If using a live chicken like my mother, twist the chicken's neck using your two forefingers until you hear it break. Hang the chicken upside down by its feet to bleed out.

Boil a large pot of water and dunk the chicken twice while holding its legs to loosen feathers. Carefully pluck all the feathers. Remove the head for another use. Cut open belly and remove organs. Rinse out body cavity. Cut chicken in half. (We always hoped to see little baby egg yolks attached to the inside of the cavity.) Reserve giblets and intestine for soup.

Place intestines in salt water, slice open with scissors lengthwise. Rinse carefully several times, cut and tie into knots. Clean giblets and rinse off the organs.

Place chicken, giblets and other organs and intestine in a large pot with enough cold water to cover by two inches. Bring to a boil and carefully skim the foam and fat off the top. Simmer over low heat. After 30 minutes, add carrots, celery, onions, garlic, cheese rind, bay leaf, salt, pepper and tomato. Simmer slowly for one hour or more, until all items are soft and fully cooked and the broth is slightly reduced. Pull chicken meat from bones. Season as needed.

Pastas used for the soup would include acini di pepe, farfalline, capellini, homemade quadrucci and tagliolini. Serves the whole family.

Cuccia (Wheat Berries with Honey)

Cuccia is traditionally served on St. Lucy's Day on December 13th and again in May. St. Lucy is the patron saint of eyes.

3 cups wheat berries

½ tsp. salt

Honey, to taste

Ground cinnamon, to lightly sprinkle on top.

Soak wheat berries in water overnight. Drain. Put wheat berries in a pot and cover with water by an inch or two and bring to a boil. Lower heat and continue to cook for 30 to 40 minutes. Drain if necessary and add the honey and cinnamon. Serves 12.

Fresh Fava Bean Sauce

3 lbs. fresh green fava beans, shelled

1 small onion, diced

2 tbsp. olive oil

1 tsp. salt

1 cup pasta water, more or less as needed to achieve desired consistency

1½ lbs. homemade pappardelle

Heat a pot of water large enough to hold all the beans. Remove beans from shell pods. Blanch beans for three minutes. Pour out into strainer. Peel skin off the beans and place in bowl.

Heat a shallow saucepan over medium heat. Add olive oil, onions and salt. Sauté until soft. Add in fava beans. Sauté for five minutes. Add a little pasta water. Simmer for five to ten minutes. Lightly mash with the back of a fork till sauce is lightly textured.

Cook pappardelle until al dente. Drain pasta and place on platter. Pour sauce over the top and serve immediately with parmigiano or Romano cheese. Serves 12.

St. Joseph's Day Pasta

Fresh sardines, de-boned, or 1 tin, canned sardines

4 fresh anchovy fillets, fresh or canned

2 oz. raisins, chopped fine

2 oz. pine nuts, chopped

1 fennel bulb, diced

3 whole tomatoes, diced, skin removed

½ tsp. sugar

1 small onion, diced

3 cloves garlic, chopped

½ tsp. salt

Pinch of pepper

1 cup breadcrumbs, lightly toasted

½ tsp. fennel seeds, crushed with rolling pin

3 tbsp. olive oil

2 lbs. spaghetti or bucatini

Heat olive oil over low heat in a large pot. Add onions and sauté for two minutes. Add in garlic, sauté for two more minutes until light brown. Add in anchovies and sardines and stir. Add fresh fennel, chopped raisins, pine nuts, tomatoes, sugar, salt and pepper. Simmer with a covered lid for one hour until all ingredients have formed into a thick paste.

In a frying pan over low heat, rub the pan with olive oil. Add breadcrumbs and fennel seed and toast lightly while constantly stirring until golden brown. Be careful not to burn.

Cook pasta in boiling, lightly salted water. Drain pasta and place in serving bowl. Top with sauce and finish with breadcrumb mix. Serves 12.

Groundhog Spezzatino

1 whole groundhog, with bones, skin and organs removed

2 whole onions, peeled, diced

4 cloves garlic, chopped

1 lb. potatoes, peeled and quartered

8 fresh tomatoes, chopped

2 large carrots, chopped into 1-inch pieces

1 tsp. salt, or to taste

½ tsp. pepper

¼ cup red wine, homemade if you have it

3 tbsp. olive oil

1 tsp. fresh rosemary, or ¼ tsp. dried

1 tsp. fresh oregano, or ¼ tsp. dried

2 bay leaves

Carefully clean groundhog, removing and discarding all fur and innards. Chop into two-inch pieces with a large cleaver. In a large pot, heat the olive oil. Season meat with salt and pepper. Add to pot and brown pieces until golden. Remove from pot.

Add more oil. Sauté onions for two minutes, add garlic and sauté for one more minute until soft. Add in tomato paste and cook for three minutes. Add in all other ingredients and add enough water to almost cover. Cover with a lid and simmer for two hours until meat is tender. Serve with pasta. Serves 12.

Meatballs

1 ½ lbs. ground veal, medium grind

1 ½ lbs. ground pork, medium grind

¾ cup breadcrumbs, or dried leftover bread

½ cup Romano cheese

3 cloves garlic, crushed with mortar or minced

2 whole eggs

1 tsp. salt, or to taste

½ tsp. pepper

½ bunch Italian parsley, chopped coarsely

2 cups vegetable oil (approximately) for frying

Mix cheese and breadcrumbs together first. Place meat in a large bowl. Add breadcrumb and cheese mixture, salt, pepper, garlic and parsley. Mix evenly. Add the eggs and continue to mix until even. If mixture is too dry, add a little water, or, if too wet, add a little bit of breadcrumbs. Cook a small sample in a hot, small frying pan to check seasoning. Add salt and pepper if needed.

Using a small quantity of vegetable oil or olive oil on your hands, shape meatballs into two-ounce pieces or to your desired size.

Heat a frying pan with ½- to 1-inch of oil until hot. Carefully place meatballs into hot oil. Turn occasionally to brown evenly. Place in a colander over a tray to drain. Repeat until all the meatballs are done. Add the meatballs to simmering sugo and cook for at least one hour. Put meatballs in a bowl and serve alongside a platter of pasta topped with sugo. Serves 12.

Pasta e Fagioli

1 lb. dried brown lentils or chickpeas

1 large onion, diced

4 cloves garlic, chopped

6 fresh tomatoes, crushed

2 cups tubettini or ditali pasta

½ cup Romano cheese, or to taste

3 cups pasta water

¼ cup olive oil

1 tsp. salt

½ tsp. pepper

Soak dried beans for 24 hours in a large pot of water. Drain. In a large pot, add lentils or chickpeas to five times as much cold water. Bring to a boil. Slowly simmer until lentils or chickpeas are soft (30-40 minutes).

In another pot, bring water to a boil with a little salt. Cook tubettini until al dente, about seven minutes. Drain, but reserve some pasta water for finishing the dish.

Heat another pot over medium heat. Add in onions, garlic and crushed tomatoes. Sauté until soft. Add in lentils or chickpeas and pasta, along with enough pasta water to make it soupy. Season with salt and pepper if needed.

Ladle into bowls and top with grated Romano cheese.

Tastes even better the next day! Serves 12.

Polenta

5 cups cornmeal (coarse)

18 to 20 cups water

2 tsp. salt

⅓ cup olive oil

Sugo

In a large pot, bring water and salt to a boil over medium high heat. Slowly add the cornmeal. (Pa stirs and Mamma pours cornmeal in slowly: *"Piano, piano"*) Stir constantly until it returns to a boil. Reduce heat and cook for about an hour while stirring frequently. Be careful, as large bubbles that burst could burn your hands.

When polenta is cooked, stir in the olive oil and season with salt, if needed, and black pepper. Pour polenta over a large enamel tabletop (or wooden board), spreading it evenly to 1½-inches thick. Top with "salsiccia duro" sauce and let it cool until it sets (10 minutes), then cut into 4-inch squares. Each piece gets topped with a piece of sausage. Take a fork and slide a square in front of each family member.

Once we finished a square, we were allowed to pull another square towards us until the polenta slowly disappeared from the table.

Thinly sliced salsiccia duro (homemade hard sausage) would be added to Mamma's classic tomato sauce and slowly simmered.

Quantities may vary depending on the type of cornmeal used; thin with water, thicken with more corn meal. Serves 12.

Spareribs with Savoy Cabbage

2 lbs. pork spareribs, cut into pieces

1 large Savoy cabbage, roughly chopped

1 large onion, diced

4 cloves garlic, crushed

4 tomatoes, chopped

6 potatoes, quartered

3 tbsp. olive oil

3 sprigs flat leaf parsley, chopped

Salt and pepper, to taste

Heat the oil in a high-sided pot on medium high heat. Salt the ribs and brown on both sides. Reduce heat to medium, remove meat and all but three tablespoons of oil. Add onions and garlic and sauté for a few minutes. Add tomatoes and cook for approximately ten minutes. Add spareribs and cook for about ten more minutes, then add cabbage and potatoes and a little more salt and pepper.

Bring to a slow simmer, cover and cook for about an hour until the meat is very tender. Add parsley and serve. Serves 12.

Sugo

16 plum tomatoes, preserved or fresh, or 2 28-oz. canned, chopped

¼ cup, tomato paste, preserved or canned

3 tbsp. olive oil

2 small onions, peeled and diced

4 cloves garlic, crushed with mortar

2 tsp. salt

½ tsp. pepper

6 basil leaves

1 bay leaf

¼ tsp. baking soda, if needed to reduce acidity

Heat a large thick-bottomed pot over medium heat. Add oil and sauté onions for two minutes, add garlic and cook until soft and lightly coloured.

Add in tomato paste, cook for three minutes. Add tomatoes, salt, pepper, bay leaf and a cup of water. Slowly simmer for one hour, stirring occasionally, until tomatoes have broken down and sauce is evenly textured.

Taste sugo; if too acidic, add the baking soda and simmer for 15 minutes. Remove from heat and add whole basil leaves. Add browned meat at this time if using. Meatballs, sausage and spareribs were used most often. Occasionally other meats were used, including pig's tails, neck bones, pork hock, beef chunks and braciole. When my grandfather went hunting for groundhog, my mother would add it to the sugo. Serves 12.

Cucidati (Fig Cookies)

Filling:

3 packages dried figs, 250g each

1 orange, zest and juice

¼ tsp. allspice, ground

8 ounces liquid honey

Pinch of black pepper

Pastry dough:

4 cups all-purpose flour

½ lb. shortening

2 tbsp. sugar

½ cup water, or enough to form a stiff dough

Preheat oven to 350 degrees. Cut off any hard stems on the figs and discard. Grind the figs and place into a large bowl. Add the orange zest and juice, honey, allspice, black pepper and a little hot water to soften the mixture. Stir with wooden spoon until all the ingredients are mixed well (or process all the filling ingredients in a food processor). Set aside.

Mix flour and sugar together in a large bowl, add the shortening, and work it into the flour mixture with your fingers until it is evenly blended. Knead lightly until it is well combined. Dough should be stiff but workable. Chill and let rest for ½ hour.

Measure out a small handful of dough and roll it out into a thin rectangle four inches by seven inches.

Measure out a small handful of the fig mixture. Roll it into a cylinder and place it along the length of the pastry dough. Fold the dough over the sides to enclose the filling, overlapping the edges slightly. Pinch the edges together to seal.

Turn the dough seam-side down and, with a sharp knife, slice into three or four pieces. Form the pieces into S-shapes and make a series of decorative slashes about ½ inch apart and/or decorative motifs (leaves, flowers, etc.).

Bake in a preheated oven for 30 to 40 minutes or until lightly golden.

CPSIA information can be obtained
at www.ICGtesting.com
Printed in the USA
BVHW020214080222
628186BV00008B/108